STUDIES IN ENGLISH LITERATURE

Volume LVII

DREAMS
IN SEVENTEENTH-CENTURY
ENGLISH LITERATURE

by

MANFRED WEIDHORN

1970

MOUTON

THE HAGUE · PARIS

LIBRARY OF CONGRESS CATALOG CARD NUMBER: 70-106459

Printed in The Netherlands by Mouton & Co., Printers, The Hague.

Dedicated to
the memory of
Professor Moses Hadas
and to all
my other teachers
living or dead

PREFACE

Since the advent of Freud we have become highly conscious of our dreams. Nearly every educated person fancies himself capable of detecting in them a buried dislike of his loved ones or a sexual significance in round or oblong objects. The intimate, eerie, incommunicable characteristics of dreams have been brusquely converted by theorists into a universal language of the emotions, a language to be readily understood by anyone possessing the right dictionary.

Lest we take this new knowledge to be an exclusive discovery of our age, we should remember that dreams have been studied and domesticated – with our zeal if not our thoroughness – throughout history in all parts of the world. In fact, only during the short period from the seventeenth to the late nineteenth centuries were dreams scorned by Western intellectuals as otiose phenomena of no significance to anyone. In antiquity and the Middle Ages, on the contrary, dreams were thought worthy the serious attention of philosophers and theologians; were analyzed by doctors in quest of diagnosis and cure, by marketplace soothsayers desiring answers to clients' practical problems; and were used by writers in various ways in important literary works. Our new knowledge is but a restitution, making respectable a primitive superstition by dressing it in the cloak of science.

It is the literary rather than the philosophical aspect of the subject that most interests me. The great writers of the West – Homer, Herodotus, Aeschylus, Virgil, Dante, Tasso – freely used dreams in their works and were thereby part of a continuing tradition; the later writers were conscious of their predecessors' achievement. With these facts in mind, it is the object of the present study to see how dreams were made use of by writers in the great age of English literature, especially by Shakespeare and Milton.

The first two chapters serve as an introduction to the theme proper. In order to establish the intellectual background to the dreams found in literary works, I review in Chapter I the principal Western theories of the dream and their survival into the seventeenth century. This sketch provides us with a sense of what philosophers, doctors, theologians, astrologers, and essayists made of dreams at the time that contemporary poets and prose writers used them. In the second chapter I examine the kinds of dreams common to various literary genres and trace the conventional patterns that developed down the ages. In the matter of dreams, as in other intellectual fields, the seventeenth-century writers were conscious of the classical background and of the developing tradition; Eve's dream in *Paradise Lost*, for example, is indirectly related to Agamemnon's in Book II of the *Iliad* through the latter dream's numerous and changing progeny.

The three succeeding chapters examine, in the order used in Chapter II, the seventeenth-century contributions to the traditional dream genres: the heuristic dream in dream-vision works, the love dream in lyrics, the ominous mantic dream in drama, and the supernatural monitory dream in narrative works. The final chapter serves both as a review and a climax, for, besides using nearly all the traditional genres, Milton created in Eve's dream one of the most beautiful, subtle, and credible dreams in literature.

In undertaking this project I have studied with care the basic works of Freud (and of several Freudians) on the subject. I have, however, decided against applying to dreams in earlier literature his interesting but overly systematic findings. The Freudian approach to literary works has been much used and abused. Perhaps the psychoanalysis of dreams should be handled by professionals only and confined to the couch and clinic. My aim has been, rather, to see what the seventeenth-century writers were *consciously* attempting to do with what they understood dreams to be, in the light of traditional beliefs and literary uses of the dream. But this self-imposed limitation does not forbid me to glance at Freud on the few occasions when earlier theory seems to anticipate his ideas or – to put it the other way around – when he iterates an old insight.

Furthermore, my major concern has been to see how the individual dream functions within the overall construction of a literary work, and not as a psychological fact. I have for that reason not dealt with dreams in the private lives of seventeenth-century persons. The dream has been commonly used as a literary device because it offers the poet a ready way to rearrange reality, to present things that cannot take place in actuality, or to account for strange actions by a sort of "as if" statement. The function of the dream thus approaches the function of metaphor. Hence neither the theories of philosophers and psychologists nor the observations of actual dreams will be as important in the examination of individual dreams in literature as will be considerations of rhetoric, literary structure and tradition.

In closing, I wish to thank Dr. Marjorie Hope Nicolson, under whose guidance this study began to take shape; the late Dr. Moses Hadas, who read and helpfully criticized the portions dealing with antiquity; Dr. Elizabeth S. Donno and Dr. Joseph A. Mazzeo, whose observations and perceptions helped bring order to this welter of dreams.

TABLE OF CONTENTS

I

MAJOR THEORIES OF THE DREAM FROM HOMER TO HOBBES

Man is by nature curious about his future. Primitive, ancient, and medieval people readily resorted to countless methods of divination to satisfy their curiosity. It comes as no surprise, therefore, to find that all primitive folk believed in revelation through dreams and that the early theologians and physicians corroborated the popular beliefs.[1] Of interest are the various theories about the nature of this experience and about the procedure used in interpreting individual dreams. I will survey first the traditional belief in supernatural objective and in heuristic self-generated dreams, examine next the rise of naturalistic and skeptical explanations of the process, and conclude with a glance at the ancient methods of interpreting allegedly prophetic dreams.

A. SUPERNATURAL OBJECTIVE DREAMS

When, in the first book of the *Iliad,* the plague strikes the Greek camp, Achilles urges Agamemnon to find out the cause, whether through prophet, priest, or even dream interpreter, since "dreams, too, are sent by Zeus". This remark intimates that dream interpreters were regarded with sufficiently high seriousness to be mentioned alongside the important prophetic priesthoods of early Greek religion: omen interpreters and animal sacrifice interpret-

---

[1] See the following works for a discussion of dreams in primitive life: A. Bouché-Leclerq, *Histoire de la divination dans l'antiquité* (Paris, 1879), I, 278; George Sarton, *Introduction to the History of Science* (Baltimore, 1927-1947), III, 1103; N. Vaschide and H. Pieron, "Prophetic Dream in Greek and Roman Antiquity", *The Monist,* XI (1901), 186.

ers.[2] It also reminds us that the earliest dream theories – Chaldean, Egyptian, Hebrew, Greek – stressed the role of the supernatural. The Bible, for example, depicts dreams clearly inspired by God or angels; dreams explicitly prophetic; dreams that warn, order, or guide. Indeed God indicated that he would appear to all prophets other than Moses in a vision or a dream. When Saul, after falling from grace, inquired of God how to act in the face of the resurgent Philistines, "God answered him not, neither by dreams, nor by Urim [magical breastplate], nor by the prophets." These, then, were the three legitimate ways – like the three in the *Iliad* – of communicating with God.[3]

According to E. R. Dodds, the Greeks were imbued with a sense of the supernatural's role in life.[4] Hesiod speaks of sicknesses, troubles, and anxieties sent by the gods at night to haunt us.[5] Pythagoras asserts that the air is full of souls dispatching dreams to us as signs of future health or disease.[6] There was nothing "diabolic" about these spirits. They were merely the messengers of the gods and not necessarily hostile to men. Socrates eventually transformed the belief in their existence into that of a personal *daimon,* a sort of lofty spiritual guide and conscience. But concurrently, in the period between the *Odyssey* and the *Oresteia,* the daemons appeared to draw closer to man, to grow more persistent, insidious, and sinister.[7]

In the Christian era, the Church Fathers, often ignoring the problem of reconciling the existence of recalcitrant devils with

---

[2]   Homer, *The Iliad,* trans. S. Butler (New York, 1942), Bk. I, 1. 63. The interpretation is by W. S. Messer, *The Dream in Homer and Greek Tragedy* (New York, 1918), p. 7.
[3]   Num. xii. 6-8; I Sam. xxviii. 15. Similarly the Psalmist often speaks of God's visitation and instruction by night: Ps. xvii. 3; xvi. 7; xlii. 8. The strongest expressions of this belief are found in the Book of Job (e.g., iv. 13-21); even nightmares are part of God's plan (vii. 13-5; xxxiii. 14-18).
[4]   E. R. Dodds, *The Greeks and the Irrational* (Berkeley, 1956), p. 17; see also on this, Bouché-Leclerq, I, 279.
[5]   Hesiod, *Works and Days,* trans. R. Lattimore (Ann Arbor, 1959), 11. 100-105, 175-180.
[6]   Diogenes Laertius, *Lives of the Eminent Philosophers,* trans. R. D. Hicks (London, 1950), II, 347-349.
[7]   For the "Archaic Age" and Socrates see Dodds, pp. 40, 42, 57 n. 70.

that of an omnipotent God, gloried in the tableau of the human soul as the battleground of Good and Evil. Hence the pagan *daimones* or *immortales animi*, morally disinterested "spirits of the air", were replaced by malevolent devils. Homer's story of the deluding dream sent Agamemnon by an amoral Zeus was transformed in Christian literature into a dream experienced by a man of God and caused by an immoral demon in an attempt to ruin the divine plan and order.[8] The infernal forces frequently use the dream because, as St. Augustine believes, they are able to feign divine apparitions; utilizing this power in illusory visions, they turn sleep, the last resort from pain, into nightmares.[9]

St. Gregory the Great asserts that through dreams the Devil either elevates the soul with hope – so that lovers of the present life are given promises of success here – or sinks with dread those who fear misfortune, by showing them dream predictions of worse to come. Satan's aim, in either case, is to disturb the balance of incautious souls.[10] According to St. Thomas Aquinas, Satan darkens man's reason by appearing during sleep in the form of the soul of a saint or of a damned or living person. Sometimes Satan reveals the future to those in compact with him; his major purpose, however, when generating dreams in a good Christian is to discover the man's weakness in order to lead him into sin in his waking actions.[11]

Many Renaissance and seventeenth-century writers continue to assign the Devil responsibility for some of our dreams.[12] Him-

---

[8]   See chapters II, V, and VI for the development of such a dream tradition, from Homer to *Paradise Lost*, through Virgil, Tasso, Camoëns, Spenser, *et al;* and for a fuller treatment, my "Eve's Dream and the Literary Tradition" in the 1967 *Tennessee Studies in Literature*.

[9]   *The City of God*, trans. D. B. Zema and G. G. Walsh (New York, 1949), XVIII, xviii; VIII, xvi.

[10]   *Morals on the Book of Job*, trans. anon. (Oxford, 1844), pp. 449-450.

[11]   *Summa Theologica*, trans. Fathers of the English Dominican Province (New York, 1947-1948), pp. 949, 545, 557. The relevance of this Thomist notion to *Paradise Lost* is discussed in Chapter VI, Section C.

[12]   See e.g., James I of England, *Daemonologie*, ed. G. B. Harrison (London, 1924), pp. 41, 74-5; *Malleus Maleficarum*, trans. M. Summers (London, 1928), p. 50; for summaries of Renaissance works see A. H. Thorndike, *A History of Magic and Experimental Science* (New York, 1923-1958), IV, 293, 325; VI, 481; VII, 358; VIII, 513, 535. But Reginald

self a spirit, he insinuates himself into men's bodies, vitiates their health, and terrifies their souls with fearful dreams and fancies. Incubi and succubi are among the shapes he assumes to trap people by visions. Burton even attributes the early medieval Catholic visions of Heaven, Purgatory, and Hell to the force of man's uncontrolled imagination coincident with the Devil's power of deceiving.[13] When compiling in the first book of the *Pseudodoxia Epidemica* a Baconian list of the causes of human error, Sir Thomas Browne adds a non-Baconian item: the endeavors of Satan. By working through "the delusion of dreams and the discovery of things to come in sleep", Satan prompted the ancients seeking messages to lodge within temples. In this way Satan perverted for his own purposes a legitimate means of revelation established by God. The existence of diabolical dreams is, however, also an argument, according to Browne, for the reality of angelic visions. Indeed one of Satan's special deceits is to make men think that apparitions are only "melancholy bereavements of fantasy"; in this way he undermines the true apparitions of divine dreams and arouses doubts as to his own existence. A skeptical attitude to dreams is thus itself a work of Satan.[14]

The persistence through the seventeenth century of the belief in the explicitly supernatural dream is seen most clearly in the activities of some of the notable religious leaders. To be sure, not all of them in that age of religious ferment were responsive to dreams. The moderate Puritan Richard Baxter, for example, has little to say on this subject in his autobiography. But the man who dissented from Protestant dissenters, the Quaker George

---

Scot dissents, claiming that even putative diabolic dreams are really caused by the black vapours of melancholy men and not by supernatural agency (*The Discoverie of Witchcraft*, ed. M. Summers [Bungay, 1930], X, v).

[13]   Robert Burton, *The Anatomy of Melancholy*, ed. Floyd Dell and Paul Jordan Smith (New York, 1927), pp. 174, 648, 878, 880, 893; on nightmares see Thomas Nashe, *The Terrors of the Night* in *Works*, ed. R. B. McKerrow (London, 1958), III, 345-48.

[14]   Sir Thomas Browne, *Works*, ed. Geoffrey Keynes (London, 1928-1931), II, 151; V, 183. At the other extreme from Browne, Scot feels that Satan deludes people into thinking that he has God-like powers of arousing dreams (*Discoverie*, X, v).

Fox, was a man of many visions. His Journal depicts him as making his way in a hostile world with his "Friends" and his dreams, rather like a Puritan Aeneas.[15]

B. SELF-GENERATED HEURISTIC AND MANTIC DREAMS

Concurrent with the acceptance of objective dreams was the belief in a self-generated subjective dream. Primitive man had no clear concept of consciousness as a state of the "soul". The difference between dream- and waking-consciousness was therefore vague. Since the experience the soul encounters in dreams is not undergone by the body, it was assumed that the soul left the body and experienced the dream-events elsewhere; here was evidence that the soul could escape, in an "ecstasy", from the bond with the body.[16]

The theory of the self-generated dream was apparently not fully developed until the rise of the Orphic cults in the sixth and fifth centuries B.C. The complex of Orphic-Pythagorean ideas included belief in resurrection or transmigration of souls, in a consequently separate existence of the soul from the body – a dualism wherein the soul was the prisoner of the tomb-like body. Psychic and bodily activity were alleged to vary inversely, so that the psyche was most active when the body was least so. Sleep became the time of soul-awakening, of converse with heaven. The Orphic view engendered a new sense of a "subjective" dream experience not at all divine but caused by the innate occult powers of the soul liberated by sleep.[17]

Such a philosophy of dreams, part of new cultural patterns, is reflected in the writers of the classical age – Pindar, Aeschy-

---

[15] For his dreams see George Fox, *Journal*, ed. J. L. Nickalls (Cambridge, 1952), pp. 9, 33, 104, 119, 312, 428, 658, 663.
[16] This paragraph is based on G. S. Brett, *A History of Psychology* (London, 1912), I, 10.
[17] This paragraph is based on *ibid.*, 23, and A. Leo Oppenheim, *The Interpretation of Dreams in the Ancient Near East* ("Transactions of the American Philosophical Society", New Series, Vol. XLVI, Part 3; Philadelphia, 1956), p. 237.

lus, Xenophon, et al.[18] Thus Plato's "Timaeus" contains a physiological explanation of the dream process and a justification of heuristic dreams. In order to check evil images and phantasms, God put into the lower soul a mirror-like power to reflect thought. This faculty is a second phantasy, able to produce images of the higher soul's contemplation of ideal objects. It supplants the normal phantasy and, dwelling in the liver, terrorizes the natural desires resident there. When the understanding begets gentle phantasms, the liver attains restful sleep and practices divination in dreams, without mind or reason.[19]

This analysis suggests that the rational soul's intellectual insights are perceived as images by the irrational soul and that the dream experience has an indirect relation to reality. The power of thought commands sympathetic activity in the liver, so that we not only know something to be bad but feel disgust at it. Dreams thus reflect in the lower nature truths arrived at by the higher soul and enable us to have personal experience of the absolute through the senses.[20]

---

[18]   See Pindar, Odes, trans. Sir John Sandys (London, 3rd ed., 1937), p. 591; Aeschylus, "Eumenides", 11. 104-105, in Plays, trans. D. Grene and R. Lattimore (New York, n.d.); Xenophon, Cyropaedia, trans. Walter Miller (Cambridge, Mass., 1947), viii. 7.
[19]   Plato, "Timaeus", 70-72, in Dialogues, trans. B. Jowett (New York, 1937), II, 49-50.
[20]   This paragraph is based on Murray W. Bundy, The Theory of the Imagination in Classical and Medieval Thought (Urbana, 1927), pp. 51-52, 258.

In spite of his elaborate explanation of heuristic and mantic dreams, Plato evinces in some passages a skepticism as to the whole matter. His alternative analysis of dreams is in terms of the internal motions of the body. At the time of the creation of man, the inner movement was violent, hindering the soul from predominating. When the flood of growth and nutriment abated and became steadier, the revolutions were corrected, the soul's courses regained their proper motions, and the individual became a rational creature. These motions remain a continual threat, however, especially to the pure internal fire that is related to the external light of everyday. Knowledge results from the combination of the light of the eyes with the external light. When the latter disappears at night, the eyelids close to keep in the internal fire, which then equalizes the inward motions, providing rest in the absence of sense experience and allowing the soul to sleep. If the rest is profound enough, sleep is undisturbed by dreams; should the great motions remain, they engender dreams that vary with the nature

This theory was adopted as well by the Stoics, especially Posidonius. In sleep, the body lies as dead; the soul, withdrawn from contact with it and freed from worldly cares for the pure activities of reason, is alive and strong. It recalls the past, comprehends the present, foresees the future. Having lived from eternity, it sees in sleep all that exists in nature, converses with other souls without the intervention of eyes, ears, tongue – as do the gods. Since the sundering of body and soul is most complete in death, the power of divination is much enhanced by the approach of dissolution.[21]

The Stoics regarded oneiromancy of any kind as ultimately traceable to divine benevolence, or to Fate, that is, the orderly succession of cause and effect. Aware of the existence of worthless quacks and superstitious fortune-tellers, they claimed that the art could not be judged by the prostitutions of it. They like-

---

and locality of the motion (Plato, "Timaeus" 43-46 in *Dialogues*, II, 24-26).

Here then is a physiology which prefers the dreamless state. This attitude is enlarged upon in the *Republic* in terms of psychology. The unlawful appetites in everyone are usually controlled by reason; when reason and the ruling power are asleep, however, the desires remain awake: "The wild beast within us, gorged with meat or drink, starts up and having shaken off sleep, goes forth to satisfy his desires; and there is no conceivable folly or crime – not excepting incest or any other unnatural union, or parricide, or the eating of forbidden food – which at such a time, when he has parted company with all shame and sense, a man may not be ready to commit." Even in good men the wild-beast nature peers out in sleep, while the tyrannical man soon goes on to commit in reality what he had only dreamed of so far (Plato, "The Republic" 571 in *Works*, I, 829-830). G. S. Brett believes that if the Orphic-Pythagorean vein in Plato caused him to posit no unity of body and soul, but only a mode of waking co-existence, with the soul trying to work out its separation and salvation by reason and mantic dreams, the same influence may well have suggested that other dreams represent the interference of bodily functions with the soul (Brett, I, 97).

Plato takes a dour view of dreams elsewhere as well. In the *Apology*, he speaks of death as a deep sleep without dreams, the most pleasant sleep to be had (Plato, I, 422); in the *Laws*, he recommends that those who are terrified by nightmares should obtain remedies in the temples because the superstitious are easily abused by dreams (II, 651). What then was Plato's final position? For various explanations of his ambivalent response to dreams, see Dodds, pp. 185, 217; Bundy, pp. 53-54; Brett, I, 71.

[21] Posidonius is discussed in Cicero, *De senectute. De amicita. De divinatione*, trans. W. A. Falconer (London, 1923), pp. 91, 295-97, 343, 349, 365.

wise dissociated divination from determinism: unfavorable prophecies do not cause what subsequently occurs but merely foretell
what will occur unless precautions are taken.[22]

Zeno is reported by Plutarch to have held that a man's progress
in virtue could be gauged by the growing cleanliness of his
dreams; such alteration bears witness to the predominance of
reason over passion. Deriving this belief from Plato's remark
that men will commit even incest in dreams, Plutarch explains
that, just as a well-trained beast behaves well when freed, a
properly disciplined soul acts nobly in sleep. Bad dreams occur
to those whose unregenerate souls feel free to revel in passion
during slumber.[23]

However, the most detailed and complicated justification of
the self-generated dream comes to us from a Neoplatonist, Synesius of Cyrene (ca. A.D. 400). He asserts that the soul, able to
comprehend Being only through impressions from phenomena,
has to employ the imagination (*phantasia, pneuma*) to communicate with Mind. We know the supra-sensible reality in terms of
sensible experience, thanks to the imagination, which is incorporeal and without a separate organ of sense. We cannot aban-
don the imagination and reach pure intellect – the knowledge
removed from sense perception and opinion, Plato's *noesis* –
but the dream state comes closest to doing so, because the sense
faculties are in abeyance.[24]

Surprisingly the veridical nature of the dream Synesius explains
somewhat in the fashion of the materialism of Democritus. Images flow from all things that are, were, or will be. The imagination is a mirror to these images, which are otherwise unseen.
Those of existing things are distinct, of future events less so. The
latter images are "riddles of closely stored seeds", advance waves
from the not-yet existent. This process is rendered possible by the
sympatheia in the world organism, whose parts belong to each
other as the limbs of one body and respond as the strings of a

[22] *Ibid.*, pp. 251, 259, 361-63, 369.
[23] Plutarch, *Moralia,* trans. F. C. Babbitt (London, 1927), I, 441-45.
[24] Synesius, *Essays and Hymns,* trans. A. Fitzgerald (London, 1930), pp.
81, 98, 331, 335.

lyre. Events in the stellar system stir vibrations in the individual mind, which is an integral part of the universal Mind. In sleep we have a pledge of divinity through dreams that raise the imagination from participation in the lower category of perception to the life of the pure mind, to the idea in its immaterial form; we approximate then the pure life of the soul after death.[25]

Established in antiquity, the tradition of the self-generated dream persists through the Middle Ages and the Renaissance largely unchanged by Christian doctrine. Men like St. Athanasius, St. Clement, Nemesius of Emesa, Prudentius, and Paracelsus, Rabelais, and Timothy Bright casually refer to the belief as to an undisputed fact.[26] Although this tradition declines in the seventeenth century, Thomas Tryon advances it with undiminished confidence and elaborateness: when the body is in its natural passivity at night, the soul is free to dream, that is, to shake off the fetters of the senses, to be on the wing "in the suburbs of Eternity", to visit "remote countries" and "celestial spheres", where essential joy and sorrow are available to it. It has secret intercourse with spirits in the "wonderful communications" of God with his servants through dreams and visions.[27]

---

[25] *Ibid.*, pp. 79-80, 328, 346, 350-51. The idea of *sympatheia*, an old Stoic motif (W. Lang, *Das Traumbuch des Synesius* [Tübingen, 1926], pp. 34-5), survived for a long time. It is found in works written in the thirteenth century (Thorndike, III, 559), in the fourteenth century (J. H. Robinson, *Petrarch* [New York, 1901], pp. 43-46), and in the seventeenth century (Thorndike, VII, 357-58; VIII, 480). Also see Bacon, *Works,* ed. J. Spedding and E. L. Ellis (London, 1872), II, 666.

[26] See St. Athanasius, *Contra Gentes* (*Nicene and Post Nicene Fathers,* Second Series, ed. P. Schaff and H. Wace, IV, New York, 1903), 21; St. Clement of Alexandria, *Christ the Educator,* trans. S. P. Wood (New York, 1954), p. 163; Nemesius of Emesa, *On the Nature of Man,* ed. W. Telfer (Philadelphia, 1955), pp. 278, 297, 338, 344; Prudentius, trans. J. H. Thomson (London, 1949), I, 49; Paracelsus, *Selected Writings,* ed. J. Jacobi, trans. N. Guterman (Second Ed., New York, 1958), pp. 134-36; Rabelais, trans. T. Urquhart and P. LeMotteux (Oxford, 1934), II, 61-63; Timothy Bright, *A Treatise of Melancholie* (London, 1586), ed. H. Craig (New York, 1940), pp. 117-119. See also Thorndike, III, 405, 558-59; VII, 219, 296-97, 314; VIII, 505.

[27] Thomas Tryon, *A Treatise of Dreams and Visions* (London, Second Ed., 1695), pp. 3, 30-32, 74-5, 165, 177-79, 186. In his rhapsodic articulation of the soul's unique sleeping experiences, Tryon stresses the great

The idea of Tryon's which is relatively uncommon in seventeenth-century England is of the self-knowledge available through dreams:

Since the heart of Man is deceitful above all things, therefore for him that would truly know himself, it has by the wise Doctors of Morality been always advised to take notice (among other things) of his usual Dreams, there being scarce anything that more discovers the Secret bent of our minds and inclinations to Vertue and Vice, or this or that particular Evil ... than these nocturnal sallies and reaches of the soul, which are more free and undisguised, and with less reserve than such as are manifested when we are awake.[28]

We seem to be here on the verge of the Freudian theory of dreams,[29] but Tryon's words remain those of a seventeenth-century Christian. Unlike the modern interest in dreams as instruments of psychological diagnosis, Tryon's curiosity springs from an ancient moral impulse. As a revelation of the true heart of man, the dream can be the first step in the process of Christian regeneration. It is made possible because the cosmic *sympatheia* draws demons to bad men, angels to good men. Since the thoughts of most people are a necessary mingling of good and evil, the two kinds of spirits struggle within us for mastery. If the intem-

---

joys obtainable from a pleasant dream and the extreme fright from a bad one; the soul, separated from the body and undistracted by the senses or waking anxieties, experiences then essential incorporeal joy and fear (pp. 59-65, 66-67, 176).

[28]   *Ibid.,* pp. 6-7, 57.

[29]   Tryon adumbrates, in fact, also the psychoanalytic explanation of awakening. Freud holds that, when the pressures of the unconscious become so powerful that the sleeping ego can no longer ward them off or disguise them, the ego abandons its wish to sleep and returns the dreamer to waking life in a state of anxiety (*The Interpretation of Dreams,* trans. A. A. Brill [London, 1937], p. 513; *An Outline of Psychoanalysis,* trans. J. Strachey [New York, 1949], p. 56). According to Tryon, it would be terrible if a man with a frightful nightmare were unable to awake, because experiencing essential fear – for the dream presents emotions in undiluted form – would be tantamount to damnation; hence "when the Soul is thus perplexed, and in this terrible fear and horror, it violently seizes on the Body, as its Natural House, and with its fierce motion awakes it, and causes the very flesh to tremble, and then the Soul or Spirit is glad and rejoices that it hath escaped those dangers" (p. 64).

perate thoughts gain the upper hand, the lapse is signalled by vain dreams. Thus the vision reflects not merely the waking consciousness but the hidden thoughts we may not be cognizant of in our day-to-day life.[30]

Tryon's ideas are paralleled by those of another seventeenth-century writer. Owen Felltham declares: "Dreams are a notable means of discovering our own inclinations" under the mantle of night; "in sleep we have the naked and natural thoughts of our souls" without the interposition of outer objects. "None of the Cinqueports of the Isle of Man are then open, to let in any strange disturbers. Surely how we fall to Vice, or rise to Virtue, we may by observation find in our dreams." Felltham adduces Zeno's claim that he could discover a man's character by his dreams, "for then the soul, stated [sic] in a deep repose, be-wray'd her true affections: which in the busie day she would either not shew or not note". Hence dreams sometimes "call us to a recognition of our inclinations which print the deeper in such quiet time".

Having made this assertion, Felltham does not indicate just how we are to understand our dreams. He takes a cautious middle way on the question of their veracity: "Every dream is not to be regarded: nor yet are all to be cast away with contempt. I would neither be a Stoick, superstitious in all; nor yet an Epicure, considering none." On the one hand, he has faith in their reliability, because, "if the physician may by them judge the constitution of the body I see not, but the Divine may do so, concerning the Soul". On the other hand, he refuses to be more specific:

I doubt not but the genius of the Soul is waking and motive, even in the deepest sleep. But to presage from these sleepy thoughts, is a wisdom that I would not reach at. The best use we can make of dreams, is Observation; and by that our own correction, or incouragement.[31]

[30] Tryon, pp. 36-38, 46, 80-81, 88, 93, 100, 109, 156, 228. We are dealing, then, not with anticipations of Freud but with the tradition of Plato, who feels that the dream can reveal the beastly nature resident in us; of Zeno, for whom dreams are signs of self-control or lack of it; and of Synesius, whose advice that we record our dreams bespeaks a faith in their capacity to reveal something important about the dreamer's character.
[31] Owen Felltham, *Resolves: Divine, Moral, Political,* twelfth ed. (London, 1709), pp. 125-127.

His contemporary, Sir Thomas Browne, articulates a similar faith:

However dreams may bee fallacious concerning outward events, yet may they bee truly significant at home, and whereby we may more sensibly understand ourselves. Men act in sleepe with some conformity unto their awaked senses, and consolations or discouragements may bee drawne from dreams, which intimately tell us ourselves.

Hence Luther would not have been terrified by an evil spirit at night, since it could not frighten him when he was awake; Crassus must have been parsimonious in his dreams, and Antony munificent in his. These hypothetical examples Browne advances to buttress his basic supposition that dreams are, so to speak, "in character": "Persons of radicall integritie will not easily bee perverted in their dreams, nor noble minds do pitifully [sic] things in sleep". We are even "somewhat more than ourselves in our sleep".[32]

This theory, *prima facie* close to the quasi-Freudian ones of Tryon and Felltham in its emphasis on self knowledge, actually has a different import. It postulates that the dream reflects the waking – the "official" – self of the man in whom the civilized soul is in complete control of all impulses, whereas Tryon and Felltham speak rather of the hidden self lurking beneath the waking, day-to-day "official" mask we present to others. In holding that dreams directly reflect character, Browne seems closer to Pythagoras, Socrates, Zeno, and the Neoplatonists, who asserted that man could achieve satisfying dreams if he lived temperately and piously. Such a belief implies that man can master himself and his dreams – a notion present also in Tryon and Felltham (as, by necessity, in all Christian thinkers) but not so sanguinely advanced by them.

C. NATURALISTIC AND SKEPTICAL THEORIES

We have seen that the writers of the Bible occasionally assert, by precept or example, the validity of supernatural dreams. At

[32]   Sir Thomas Browne, "On Dreams" in *Works,* V, 185.

other times, however, they are skeptical on this matter. The author of Deuteronomy, for instance, commands that if prophets or dreamers follow strange gods, Israel is to destroy such men instead of heeding them. Jeremiah is most outspoken against dreams and often attacks the prophets who tell of false dreams which purport to assure peace to come. Isaiah delineates the natural wish-fulfillment dream: "It shall even be as when a hungry man dreameth, and, behold, he eateth; but he awaketh, and his soul is empty." The writer of Ecclesiastes speaks of dreams coming "through the multitude of business" – that is, caused by the waking cares of the sleeper – and adds skeptically, "in the multitude of dreams and many words there are also diverse vanities".[33]

The great moment in ancient dream theorizing, however, comes with the impact of Greek etiology.[34] The first thorough naturalistic explanation of the mechanics of dreams is made by Democritus, who thinks that they are caused by the impact during sleep of phantoms (*eidola, simulacra*) continually emanating from material bodies. Since the phantoms reproduce the mental activities of the persons whose forms they copy, some foresight is available through dreams. Furthermore, we sometimes dream of

---

[33] Deut. xiii. 1-5; Jer. xiv. 13-15; xxiii. 25-32; xxvii. 9; xxix. 8; cf. Zech. x. 2; Is. xxix. 7-8; Eccl. v. 3, 7. Even more outspokenly skeptical are the statements in Ecclesiasticus (xxxiv. 1-7; xl. 5-8). In all likelihood the ambivalence in the Bible sprang out of a desire on the part of its writers to distinguish divine mantic dreams from the impostures of false prophets as well as from the obscure vanities of casual dreams.

[34] This observation is made by Dodds, pp. 117-18. In view of the inquisitive and sometimes skeptical Greek mind, it is not surprising to find that some of the earliest explicit comments on dreams had only partly to do with the gods. A naturalistic approach is latent in remarks by Pythagoras (Diogenes Laertius, *Lives*, II, 341), Empedocles (Bundy, p. 13), Heraclitus (in Hippocrates, *Works*, trans. W. H. S. Jones [London, 1931], IV, 471, 501), Diogenes the Cynic (Diogenes Laertius, II, 27, 45). In Herodotus's story of the dream of Xerxes, we have a strange blend of old superstition and the new naturalist approach. The Persian ruler is told in a dream to invade Greece; when he informs Artabanus of it, the latter replies that the roving dreams that visit men – we note the language of the old objective dream – often spring from the thoughts of the day (*Histories*, trans. G. Rawlinson [New York, 1942], vii. 12-19).

dead people because their phantoms are still floating about.[35]

A different origin of dreams is suggested in the first extant Greek treatise on the subject, Book IV of the *Regimen* by Hippocrates. Its author draws an important distinction between the dreams of divine origin foretelling the future and requiring the knowledgeable oneiromancers to explicate and dreams of physiologic origin, by means of which the soul foretells physical symptoms and gives clues to physicians. Hippocrates then supplies a key to the interpretation of such diagnostic dreams. Those that repeat waking acts or thoughts or reveal normal sights, clothes, sizes of things show the soul to be abiding by its waking purposes and indicate bodily health. Clear landscapes, scenes of order, acts performed with assurance are also good signs. On the other hand, dreams contrary to the day's acts indicate disturbances and suggest that the body is to be treated by emetic, diet, and walks. On this general basis, Hippocrates erects a symbolism which vies with Freud's in being able to impart significance to the humblest object appearing in a dream. Visions of flood, for instance, reveal excess moisture in the body; streams refer to the bowels; monsters intimate some kind of surfeit or disease.[36]

Although the work combines fantastic notions with concrete observations, twisting facts and wildly using analogy to fit arbitrary hypotheses, it remains the first "scientific" treatment of the subject, by explaining dreams rationally and using them for diagnosis.[37] According to E. R. Dodds, it represents a break with the

---

[35]   Recorded in Cicero, pp. 507, 527. Such remarks are to be seen against the background of nearly universal belief in the supernatural qualities of dreams and of the "official" dream interpretation practiced in Greek temples from the sixth century B.C. on (Sarton, I, 89). No one, not even in the ancient Near East, denied that *some* dreams are without significance; as Ennius puts it, "aliquot somnia vera sunt sed omnia non necesse est" (*Remains of Old Latin*, trans. E. H. Warmington [London, 1935], I, 379). No criteria existed, however, to distinguish dreams by demoniac possession (worthy of trust) from the idle ones. Hence the question really raised by the rationalists was whether *any* dreams at all are significant.

[36]   Hippocrates, IV, pp. 421-25, 437-447. For Freud, as for Hippocrates, the dream symbols often refer to bodily parts, albeit mainly the genitalia (*Interpretation of Dreams*, pp. 336-40).

[37]   This observation is made by W. H. S. Jones in Hippocrates, p. lii; and by Brett, I, 49, 51, 54.

traditional Aesculapian incubation cures, by stressing the internal source of dreams rather than their divine aspect. While he concedes that prayer is useful, Hippocrates in effect secularizes the practice of dream interpretation as applied to medicine.[38]

The climax of ancient dream theorizing is reached with Aristotle's famous works on the subject. Unlike all earlier writers, he takes account of the senses' contribution to dreams. For one thing, an environmental influence persists even into the unconscious state; a small impulse from without, such as a distant sound or faint echo, may appear in the dream as thunder. But even in the case of a complete cessation of sense perception, impressions persist after the external object is gone and after the given sense has ceased to operate actively. In turning from a green object to a red one, we still see momentarily a fading green; similarly, an object may appear to exist externally when the sense is stimulated from within. We are easily deceived by such leftover stimuli, which occur both when we are awake and when asleep. In the former case they are eclipsed by the active senses and mind. As the waking movements cease, however, even small stimuli come to the surface, move in the little blood left in the senses, stir the inner organs, simulate real objects, and project images on the dreaming mind. When we are awake, the controlling common sense affirms the report of the most authoritatively impressive sense perception; in sleep this control is wanting and false sense impressions appear as true.[39]

Since Aristotle recognizes no such gulf between form and matter as obtains between Plato's Ideas and things, dreams are not necessary in his scheme for imaginative reminiscences of immutable reality. They are accounted for rather by their relation to the material world, to waking thoughts. In the face of Plato's partly lofty theory of fantasy, prophetic vision, and dreams, Aristotle explains the mental processes in sleep as analogous to waking experiences. The activity of the fantasy in dreams is conformable to the laws of experience; it is the same power that

[38] Dodds, pp. 119, 130.
[39] Aristotle, *Parva Naturalia*, trans. W. S. Hett (London, 1935), pp. 347-351, 357, 361-63.

subsists in waking thoughts but under different conditions, for sleep merely distorts the reality perceived by the sleeper as much as the love affection does that of the lover.[40]

While Plato held that inner movements cause dreams by unbalancing the rational soul, Aristotle maintains the reverse. The soul in movement – as it is in children, drunks, madmen – cannot think. Dreams come only when the mind is steady and at rest. The soul moves most in early sleep and cannot then think or dream; therefore, when heat collects within the body after food ingestion, the sleep is deepest and most pleasant. Aristotle implies thereby that the clearest dreams will take place in the morning hours, when the stomach is free of food, the body heat and movements have been dissipated, and the elements are mixed in normal balance after digestion. The veracity of the morning dream, a widespread belief in late antiquity, was to become a recurrent theme of defenders of oneiromancy down through the Renaissance.

These explanations of dreams leave Aristotle without their "final cause". Indeed when he faces the problem of whether they are God-sent, he hesitates. The fact that vivid dreams are experienced by lower animals and inferior and melancholy persons seems to show that they cannot be from God, who would send them by day and to the wisest men. Rather the evidence points the other way: dreams appear to ordinary men because their minds, vacant of thoughts, readily follow the slightest stimulus.[41] In one puzzling and debated sentence, he suggests *daemons* as a possible source because they are a part of nature.[42] At the same time he accepts the Hippocratic approach as valid: physicians rightly make dreams either causes or effects of bodily changes, for the small beginnings of diseases about to visit the body must be more evident in the sleeping than the waking state.[43] In the *Problems* Aristotle provides a bridge between the waking thoughts and the subsequent inner stirrings of sleep as he has analyzed

---

[40] This paragraph is based on Bundy, pp. 68, 76-79.
[41] Aristotle, pp. 329-331, 379-381.
[42] *Ibid.*, p. 377.
[43] *Ibid.*, p. 375.

them. When sleep overtakes a man, he is perceiving or thinking. The dream carries on in some fashion the thoughts of what he did or intended or wished to do.[44] The impact of waking thoughts and hidden desires on dreams is also recognized in the statements that dreams may rehearse an action already completed or carry through an act of which only the intention as yet exists, and that intimate friends, often thinking of each other, are likely to dream of each other.[45] In the last analysis, Aristotle parts company with both the mantic view and the Hippocratic, by suggesting that most dreams have trivial causes and are without results.

Praise has been universal for his dream theory. He was the first to articulate, however tentatively, a clear and large variety of natural causes. His three short treatises achieve occasional brilliance, such as insights into a common origin for dreams, hallucinations of the sick, and illusions of the sane. These works, with Plato's "Timaeus", were directly or indirectly the main source of the extensive medieval literature on dreams.[46]

The belief that, in the varying words of the proverb, "Träume sind Schäume", "les songes sont mensonges", is developed in a different manner by the Epicureans. According to the epistemology passed on to Lucretius from Democritus, the phantoms, images of a finer texture, affect the mind rather than the eyes, so that we are able to think of external objects not present to the senses. The atoms of the mind-spirit compound are small and quickly moved by delicate causes. The mind is consequently readily deceived awake: it sees only the images it directs its attention to; it withdraws from others, jumps to conclusions. It is even more readily deceived in sleep when we seem to be awake, to move, see, act; when the phantoms assail it to a stronger degree; when

---

[44] *Idem, Problems*, trans. W. S. Hett (London, 1937), II, 179.

[45] *Idem, Parva*, pp. 377, 381. This became a theme of the literature of dreams see especially Chapter IV, Section A. The relation of dreams to waking thoughts had been adumbrated by the early Epicureans and atomists, by Herodotus's story of Xerxes's dream, and by the Bible. Developed by Aristotle, the idea was common in late antiquity.

[46] Evaluations are made by Dodds, pp. 120, 283; Vaschide, p. 186; Sarton, I, 129. As Bundy (p. 83) points out, we have here two rival philosophies of the phantasy and dreams, one idealistic and the other empirical.

the images of a man may, for example, easily mix with that of
a horse to form a centaur; when the senses are obstructed and
cannot refute the false by the true; when memory is also asleep
and cannot tell us that the terrifying image represents a person
long dead.[47]

This analysis depicts dreams as caused by external impressions and as the product of chance. Lucretius, however, develops
concurrently a different theory – ultimately derived from Aristotle.
Whatever occupies our waking thoughts we will encounter in
dreams. Certain passages of the mind are left open through
which these images enter when we cease to observe with the
senses. Lawyers dream of law, generals of war, dogs of chase,
birds of pursuit; Lucretius himself dreams of the nature of things.
Some men even bear witness against themselves in sleep. Most
fragile of all is the young man with maturing sexual organs who,
easily aroused by chance images of a beautiful women, seems to
copulate with her in a dream. Since we tend to observe our own
wounds, the youth injured by love returns in his mind to the cause
and yearns to be united with the beloved. Lucretius is here close
to the notion of the dream as wish-fulfillment, an idea of which
antiquity – Aristotle before him, Petronius and Claudian after
him – was not unaware.[48] His ultimate view of dreams, however, is bleak. Man is a creature who seeks oblivion in sleep, as
part of a general flight from himself, but who never satisfies his
quest because of the presence of anxiety dreams.[49]

---

[47]   Lucretius, *De rerum natura,* trans. W. H. D. Rouse (London, 1924),
pp. 210, 251-279, 281, 301-305; Diogenes Laertius, II, 579. The tableau
of the Epicurean living by these principles can be seen in several literary
passages: Petronius, *Satyricon,* trans. W. Arrowsmith (Ann Arbor, 1959),
p. 112; Plutarch, *Parallel Lives,* the "Dryden" trans., (New York, n.d.),
Brutus, xxxvi-xxxvii.

[48]   Lucretius, pp. 245, 317-323, 423; Aristotle, *Problems,* p. 179; Petronius,
p. 157; Claudian, trans. M. Platnauer (London, 1922), II, 71-73. A couplet
(quoted in R. Scot, p. 102) well known in the Middle Ages – and translated
by Chaucer's Pertelote – was:

   Somnia ne cures, nam mens humana quod optat,
   Dum vigilat sperans, per somnum cernit id ipsum.

[49]   Among later classical writers, the most eloquent skeptic on this matter
is Cicero. Book II of his *De divinatione* refutes everything advanced in
the first book as part of the Stoic belief in mantic dreams. He concludes

In the Middle Ages,[50] the naturalistic explanation of dreams was propounded by physicians, astrologers, philosophers, and theologians. These writers have been studied with care by Walter Curry, who, while cognizant of differences in details among individual thinkers, has synthesized a medieval theory of dreams. As a group working in the Aristotelian and patristic traditions, they share a broad consensus, unlike the differences which separate, say, Lucretius from Synesius, or Aristotle from Artemidorus. This medieval theory has three aspects – medical, astrological, theological – the relative importance of which varies according to the discipline of the writer.

The medical explanation is bound up with the psychology of sleep. The vapor ascending to the brain from the lower members or from digesting foods causes slumber. The *virtus animalis* then withdraws from its instruments – the senses and muscles – to rest in the inner parts, allowing the *virtus naturalis* to exercise

---

his agile attack by posing the basic dilemma (which so many writers on the subject ignore): how can we distinguish mantic from idle dreams (pp. 495, 503, 507-509, 515-17, 521, 527, 533)?

[50] As we approach the later analyses of dreams, it is well to keep in mind that the period from 400 B.C. to A.D. 400, from Hippocrates and Democritus to Synesius and Macrobius, established and clarified virtually all possible positions on the dream problem. In subsequent epochs, the basic ideas of the Greeks were sometimes reshuffled; slight differences in emphases were developed; but little that was really original was asserted, at least until the revolution of the late nineteenth century.

At the same time we must recall that two cardinal beliefs of medieval dream lore – the validity of the morning dream and the interpretation by contraries – were almost unknown to classical times and first became important in late antiquity. Three things, furthermore, are clear about the post-classical dream theories. The Christian believed in mantic dreams because of the examples in Scripture, yet even the most emphatic asserters of their validity held (with possibly one exception) that some dreams were not merely idle but often the work of diabolic forces. Secondly, it was still impossible to establish a criterion distinguishing the mantic from the otiose; the need for such a criterion was often not even mentioned. Thirdly, the belief in dreams sent from without, either from the Christian God or the Devil, represented a marked resurgence of the older "objective" dream. Nevertheless, the tradition of the "subjective" dream – as a manifestation of the soul's own occult power – which we have watched emerge in classical Greece and carried on by Neoplatonists, was still vital, especially in those Fathers with Neoplatonic tendencies.

appetitive, retentive, expulsive, digestive functions and to recreate natural heat. Dreams are phantasms originating in movements of sense images in the imagination; the dreamer thinks his senses are responding to external impression even though his *virtus animalis* is withdrawn and the senses are quiescent.

The medieval doctors generally classify dreams by causes: (1) *somnium naturale:* any disturbance in the balance of bodily complexions and humours is registered in the mind as a dream; (2) *somnium animale:* anxieties of the waking mind are recorded in the imagination, and their impressions are reproduced in sleep; (3) *somnium coeleste* or *divina:* when the mind is at rest, spirits impregnate it with images of coming events. A given dream need only be classified – though that is always difficult – before we know how valid it is as a harbinger of coming events. The *somnium naturale* is false as prophecy but useful in diagnosing maladies; the *somnium coeleste* may be significant, primarily in the morning when the mind is least oppressed by humours and in best condition. The *somnium animale* is of no interest to the physicians.[51]

The astrologers use a similar classification, except that instead of the *somnium animale* caused by waking thoughts, they posit dreams due to planetary influence. These may be true, depending upon the power, position, application, and aspect of the planets at the time of the dream. To the astrologers divine dreams are true, while those caused by bodily humours are false. The theologians, on the other hand, are mainly interested in the *revelatio,* although they concede that all *somnia* are of possible significance.[52] St. Thomas Aquinas, for instance, distinguishes between dreams

---

[51] This analysis is based on W. C. Curry, *Chaucer and Medieval Science* (New York, 1926), pp. 203-208.

[52] *Ibid.,* pp. 210-211, 213-14. As Curry points out there was no basic conflict among medieval philosophers, astrologers, physicians, and theologians on dream theories; any difference was merely of emphasis. Although the physicians were concerned primarily with the *somnium naturale,* they conceded the validity of the other kinds. The philosophers and astrologers were interested in the *somnium animale* and its psychology. The theologians, while accepting the conclusions of the others on these two types, concentrated upon the *somnium coeleste,* which all men agreed to be valid heralds of the future (Curry, p. 217).

with inward causes, whether from the soul's waking thoughts or the body's disposition, and those with outward causes, whether from corporeal agents in the surrounding air and heavenly bodies, or from God through the ministry of incorporeal angels. When the dream is due to natural inward or outward causes, the divination is proper only so far as the efficacy of that cause extends; thus dreams caused by humours can reveal the physical state of the body and no more.[53] Thomas thus justifies all three aspects of the medieval dream theory. Nevertheless we are, as usual, not told how to determine in which category a given dream belongs.

Useful and relatively rare is Thomas's naturalistic analysis of the way the various kinds of dreams are formed by the degree of exhalation or evaporation of fumes. If much exhalation takes place – as a result of recent eating – not only is the intellect hindered by the suspension of sense, but the imagination's activity is curtailed as well; no dream phantasms can then occur. When less exhalation takes place, the phantasms begin to appear, although distorted and without order. Should the exhalation be slight, the phantasms will have a sequence, as often occurs among sober and imaginatively gifted people. In the case of very slight evaporation, the imagination and even the common sense are partly freed. Hence the sleeper, able to distinguish between things and images, will sometimes syllogize in sleep (albeit imperfectly) or will know that he is dreaming even while he is asleep.[54] In this way Thomas, beginning with the Aristotelian physiology of sleep and making allowance for the limited role of reason, nicely accounts for the gradations of irrational dreams.

During the Renaissance there was no major break with the medieval dream tradition, and no remarkable new theory was propounded. The older classifications continued to be common. The relative predominance of mantic, natural, or diabolic dreams was still debated. What characterized the Renaissance in this discipline, as in many others, was an enriching of the available

---

[53] St. Thomas Aquinas, *Summa Theologica*, pp. 1604-1606.
[54] The sleeper will still be deceived insofar as his common sense remains partly suspended (p. 430).

literature of the past. To the old medieval sources such as Aristotle and Macrobius were added new editions and translations of works long out of currency.[55]

In Elizabethan and Jacobean England, the naturalistic explanation of dreams was widespread. They were often attributed to waking thoughts. "A dream is nothing else", Nashe says,

> but a bubbling scum or froath of the fancie, which the day hath left undigested; or an after feast made of the fragments of idle imaginations. . . . Our thoughts, intensively fixt all the day time upon a mark we are to hit, are now and then over-drawne with such force, that they flye beyonde the mark of the day into the confines of the night.

We store in the memory the images of the things best known to us. At night some humour erects a puppet stage for these images. A man obsessed with courtly advancement or gathering money has a vulnerable imagination readily impelled onto a well-worn path by any sense impression.[56]

Diet and posture are also held responsible. Burton warns that heavy meats – dark ones like hare and venison – or cabbage, beans, peas fill the brain with "gross fumes, breed black thick blood, and cause troublesome dreams". Sleeping during the day or in an uncomfortable position will have a like effect. In all such cases, those organs which are ambassadors fail in their report and deliver lies and fables.[57] Bacon, iterating in the *De Augmentis* that dream interpretation is now "full of follies" although "laboriously handled by many writers", proceeds to give the usual naturalistic explanation in a clear and concise manner:

> At present I will only observe that it [dream theory] is not grounded upon the most solid foundation which it admits; which is, that when the same sensation is produced in the sleeper by an internal cause which is usually the effect of some external act, that external act passes into the dream. A like oppression is produced in the stomach by the vapour of indigestion and by an external weight superimposed; and therefore persons who suffer from the nightmare dream of a weight lying on them.[58]

[55] The various works are summarized in Thorndike, IV, 562; V, 143; VI, 135, 475, 480, 483, 490-491; VII, 477.
[56] Nashe, *The Terrors of the Night* in *Works*, III, 355-56.
[57] Burton, pp. 190-193, 217.
[58] Bacon, III, 368; IV, 376-77.

Many writers still believe in the venerable medical theory, according to which the "overboiling" in the stomach of any humour shapes the dream. A sanguine complexion, for example, causes happy visions. On the other hand, the sharp melancholy humour, the grossest part of the blood, casts a thick mist over the spirit, "bemasking the phantasie" and engendering misshapen objects in our imagination – dreams of terror, disgrace, sorrow, fire – which displace and mock reason. "When all is said", concludes Nashe, "Melancholy is the mother of dreams, and of all terrors of the night whatsoever."[59]

Even Sir Thomas Browne, for all of his poetic response to the subject, recognizes that most nocturnal disturbances are "natural and animal". St. Chrysostom's dream of Paul sprang from his daily reading of Paul's epistles; many dreams which are thought to be illuminations or divine visions of paradise were merely "animal" dreams engendered by the waking reflections of the pious man. The other kind of dream, the "natural", can be induced by foods that make it either turbulent or peaceful. A third factor is the presence of slight sense impressions from without or leftover impressions within the body. Browne summarizes the skeptical position in a typically poetic note:

Half our dayes wee passe in the shadowe of the earth, and the brother of death exacteth a third part of our lives. A good part of our sleepes is peeced out with visions, and phantasticall objects wherein wee are confessedly deceaved. The day supplyeth us with truths, the night with fictions and falshoods, which uncomfortably divide the natural account of our beings.[60]

The same position is summarized by Hobbes in a typically rigorous logical fashion. His renovation of the traditional theory begins with a crucial word: "imagination" he defines, not as the active faculty which reviews and reshapes material presented it by the common sense but simply as decaying or weakened phan-

---

[59]   Nashe, III, 354, 357; see also on this Bright, p. 124; Burton, pp. 152, 359; Tryon, p. 24. Cf. Samuel Butler, *Satires,* ed. R. Lamar (Cambridge, 1905), p. 200:
The prophesies of Dreams prognosticate
Mens constitutions rather than their Fate.
[60]   Sir Thomas Browne, "On Dreams", in *Works,* V, 183-184, 186.

tasms. The phantasm – or fancy (Greek *phantasia;* Latin *imaginatio*) – is what remains in the mind after the perceived object is no longer present. Dreams are the sleeping man's phantasms. Because the outer nerves and sense organs are numb, the agitation of the inner parts of the body renders clearer the phantasms.[61]

Dreams have five distinctive characteristics. In the first place, since in sleep we do not consult ourselves or look to the end, there is no orderly "discourse of thoughts", no coherence. The phantasms succeed one another as they would before an open eye that is indifferent to everything. Moreover, we dream only of what is compounded of the phantasms of past experience, there being no new motion from objects without. The dreams are nevertheless partly fictitious, because they sometimes proceed from the gradual interruption of waking phantasms in drowsy people.

Hobbes finds it hard to say how phantasms are revived in spite of the sleep of the exterior organs. In some organs the sense remains, in others not. Whatever strikes the *pia mater* may revive the phantasms still in motion in the brain; perhaps impulses from the heart engendering or accompanying, say, an appetite or aversion, reach the brain and generate phantasms. Thus anger causes heat when we are awake; conversely heat in the heart when we sleep generates anger which stirs the brain by evoking a dream-image of an enemy.

Another characteristic of dreams is that they are clearer than the imaginations of waking men because dream phantasms, freshly aroused by the internal motions, occur without the distraction of external sense. Lastly, we do not marvel at the places or things that appear in dreams. Such "admiration" is brought on by the novel and the unusual, which are evident only to those who remember former appearances. But with the memory dormant, neither fancy nor judgment can take notice of likeness and difference; all things appear as present, and without surprise to us.[62] Thus Hobbes has thoroughly and tidily explained dreams

---

[61]   Thomas Hobbes, *Elements of Philosophy* in *Selected Writings*, ed. F. J. E. Woodbridge (New York, 1930), pp. 112, 115; *Leviathan*, ed. M. Oakeshot (Oxford, 1953), pp. 9-10.
[62]   *Elements*, pp. 115-117; *Leviathan*, p. 11.

in terms of motion, without recourse to God, angels, stars, faculties, humours, bodily dispositions, or desires. At best, dreams are the rags and tatters of left-over thoughts rearranged.

Hobbes also wants to throw open to inspection the many "visions", occurring between sleeping and waking, which have not been heretofore accounted dreams. Men are too ready to take apparitions perceived in sleep not as phantasms but as things subsisting of themselves, objects outside the dreamer, "as if the dead of whom they dreamed, were not inhabitants of their own brain, but of the air, or of the heaven, or hell; not phantasms, but ghosts". Demonology naturally grows out of such confusion.[63]

This argument, part of his attack on the traditional belief in incorporeal substance, can be regarded as a milestone in the history of dream theories. It is the first clear-cut refutation, during the Christian era, of the "objective dream" theory prevalent in antiquity and the Middle Ages. Skeptical writers had attacked dreams before but, with the exception of the pagan Lucretius, had always made allowance for some supernatural dreams, at least those recorded in the Bible. While Hobbes directs his argument against pagan vision-lore, his animus towards all revelation is barely veiled. He insists that the schools should be clearing men's minds of the superstitious fears of spirits, or "prognostick from dreams", and of false prophecies:

And this ought to be the work of the schools; but they rather nourish such doctrines. For, not knowing what imagination or the senses are, what they receive, they teach: some saying that imaginations rise of themselves ... and that the good thoughts are inspired into a man by God, and evil thoughts by the Devil.

The traditional scholastic dream theory is ridiculous:

Some [scholastics] say the senses receive the species of things, and deliver them to the common sense; and the common sense delivers them over to the fancy, and the fancy to the memory, and the memory to the judgment, like handling of things from one to another, with many words making nothing understood.[64]

[63] *Leviathan*, p. 419.
[64] *Ibid.*, pp. 12-13, 195-96, 419; *Elements*, p. 117.

Stepping on hitherto sacrosanct territories of the subject and reducing the dream to a simple mechanical operation, Hobbes completely naturalizes the matter and leaves the older theoretical
constructions lying in a rubble. Dream-divination he does not
even so much as give a glance. After this, the most complete
"debunking" since Lucretius's, nothing remains of the mystery
and poetry of millenia of dreams.

D. DREAM INTERPRETATION

That dream interpretation was an important facet of ancient life
can be deduced from the existence of a special class of interpreters
in Egypt, of Aesculapian temples in Greece, and of sundry
"unofficial" analysts. From the Hippocratean symbology, as well
as Galenic practice, we infer the role it played in medicine and
"psychology". Few documents, however, have survived, and none
is as explicit and detailed as the book of Artemidorus Daldianus.
Neither a philosopher nor a theorist of dreams, he was rather a
practitioner of divination, one of the thousands who crowded the
market-places of antiquity. Furthermore, whereas the Stoics and
Neoplatonists believed in the mantic dream for the self-knowledge and metaphysical lore derivable from it and for the possibility of communication with the infinite, Artemidorus's interpretations deal quite prosaically with the dreamer's immediate prosperity: whether to marry Phryne or Laïs, whether to sell one's
stocks or not. As such, Artemidorus was the great codifier of
practical dream analysis. The existence of such a man reminds
us that the interpretation of individual dreams is a field in itself,
to be distinguished from theorizing on the nature of the dream-
process. In fact, Artemidorus's *Oneirocriticon,* which has enjoyed
a "well-deserved neglect", is mainly a source book of ancient
superstition; it is pertinent to know that its author wrote also on
auspices and palmistry. Yet he remains a rare bird for us because,
of some twenty-seven books of dream interpretation mentioned
in antiquity, his is the only one to survive.[65]

[65]   This paragraph is based on the following discussions: Russell M.

Much traveled and well aware of traditional dream lore, Artemidorus makes many pronouncements that, while seeming arbitrary, apparently spring from a conventional association of things, such as of blood and gold, or feet and slaves. He begins the book by distinguishing between the dream (*somnium*), which sketches things to come, and the nightmare (*insomnium*), which deals with present matters of body and mind. Of the former, some are "speculative", that is, direct, literal scenic representations of what will soon happen; others are "allegoric", signifying things which will take several days to be realized and require professional analysis. For example, dreams of such impossible acts as flying or floating are obviously allegorical. As a professional dream interpreter, Artemidorus bothers only with the allegorical dream.

The status of the dreamer is important; no one below the rank of captain or prince can expect a "public" dream, since only important men are free of private cares. A dream which occurs to an eminent person signifies great good or evil; to a lowly person, slight good or evil. Dreams in accord with the local mores are good, contrary to them bad. The symbols must consequently be analyzed deftly, with reference to the circumstances.[66] When we turn to the specific judgments and equations, we are faced with a laborious pseudo-science. We cannot help noticing a vein of unconscious humor arising from the very solemnity of it all; to dream, for example, of the eating of books by a schoolmaster

---

Geer, "On the Theories of Dream-Interpretation in Artemidorus", *Classical Journal*, XXII (1927), 663; Bouché-Leclerq, I, 277; B. Büchsenschütz, *Traum und Traumdeutung im Alterthum* (Berlin, 1868), p. 67.

[66] *Artemidoro Daldiano Philosofo Eccellentissimo dell'Interpretatione de Sogni*, trans. Pietro Lauro Modonese (Venetia, 1542), pp. 2, 10, 18. For additional analysis see Büchsenschütz, p. 56, and Geer, p. 664.

There are in all six groups of circumstances, which, it has been suggested, correspond to the "persona" of rhetoric: (1) *natura*: whether events in the dream are natural or not; (2) *lex*: lawful or not; (3) *consuetudo*: according to the dreamer's habitual actions or not; (4) *tempus*: the time of the dream's occurrence; (5) *ars*: the vocation of the dreamer; (6) *nomen*: the dreamer's name. The circumstances are also useful in calculating the time within which the prophecy will be fulfilled; dreams of distance or of distant objects, for instance, have their effects slowly (Artemidorus, pp. 8, 10; Bouché-Leclerq, I, 305-306).

or by those who make a living from books or eloquence signifies the sudden death of that person. Artemidorus examines dreams of sexual behavior and misbehavior with the detailed exhaustiveness of an ancient Kinsey or Freud. Other dreams seem suspiciously close to anecdotes, such as the one of entering a house of ill repute: to emerge again is a good sign, not to do so forebodes ill. Then there is the interplay of the dream of marriage signifying death, the dream of death signifying a wedding; we are again at the borderland of folk humor.[67]

As Russell Geer points out, some principles underlie Artemidorus's equations. The interpreter must establish a bridge between the dream content and reality and relate this connection to the dreamer's life. The association may be made through etymology, or cause and effect, or proverbs, myths, word quibbles, and number juggling. Another principle is that something fitting to the dreamer presages good, something inappropriate to him, although good in itself, portends ill. There is little mention, however, of interpretation by contraries.[68]

This principle is first articulated in a letter by the younger Pliny to Suetonius. Because of a bad dream, Suetonius fears the outcome of a law case in which he is involved. Pliny, promising to postpone the case, agrees with his friend but proceeds to tell of the time he himself went through with a case despite a dream which urged him not to. The point he underscores for Suetonius is that, though "dreams descend frome Jove", they may work by contraries. It is necessary for each person to recollect whether his own dreams predict directly or by the reverse.[69] Pliny here touches upon what is a subterfuge for the diviners whose interpretations are unsuccessful. The meaning by contrary is much used by writers, for faith in mantic dreams overcomes all difficulties.

The devotees of this art persisted through later periods. Such men as Achmet Ibn Sirin among the Arabs, Gregoras Nicephoras

---

[67]   Artemidorus, pp. 75, 38.
[68]   These conclusions are drawn by Geer, pp. 664-68, 669.
[69]   Pliny the Younger, *Epistles,* trans. W. Melmoth (London, 2d ed., 1957), I, 61-63.

in Byzantium, Arnauld of Villanova and Michael Scot in the West achieved renown as either practitioners of or writers on dream interpretation.[70] A popular alphabetical listing of dream symbols, *The Dreambook of Daniel,* circulated through the Middle Ages in many versions.[71] During the Renaissance, men like Rigault, Ogier Ferrier, Jerome Cardan on the Continent and Thomas Hill and William Freke in England contributed sizeable volumes on the subject.[72]

Among most English writers, however, the traditional popular methods of interpretation do not have much intellectual respectability. Burton rarely refers to the interpreters of the past and their "great volumes". Nashe is less detached:

Those that will harken any more after dreams, I refer them to Artemidorus, Synesius, and Cardan, with many others . . . [whom] I, thanke God, had never the plodding patience to reade, for if they bee no better than some of them I have perused, every weatherwise old wife might write better.

Thomas Tryon is ambivalent towards the classics in this field; of the books by Aristotle, Themistius, Artemidorus, and Cardan he says that they are large but proceed "darkly and at random", without "experience".[73]

Only Sir Thomas Browne is sympathetic. On examining some of the Biblical dreams, he finds Pharaoh wise in soliciting interpretations from his magicians because, as Egyptians, they understood the symbols and hieroglyphic notions of things.[74] In the "Letter to a Friend", Browne touches on this topic again, since the Friend had a dream of death before his own decease. In this

---

[70] On these men see N. Bland, "On the Muhammedan Science of Tâbír, or Interpretation of Dreams", *Journal of the Royal Asiatic Society* (1856), p. 119; and Thorndike, II, 329-330; VI, 453.

[71] This book is discussed by M. Hélin, *La clef des songes* (Paris, 1925), *passim.*

[72] Their works are summarized by Thorndike, VI, 453; VII, 603. See Thomas Hill, *The Most Pleasant Arte of the Interpretacion of Dreames* (London, 1576); William Freke, *Lingua Tersancta* (London, 1703).

[73] Burton, pp. 140, 466; Nashe, *Terrors of the Night* in *Works,* III, 361-62, 368-373, 382; Tryon, p. 8.

[74] Browne, "On Dreams" in *Works,* V, 184-85.

case, Browne the physician confines himself to one kind of interpretation – the Hippocratean – in an approach that is cautiously scientific. "From the thoughts of sleep, when the soul was conceived nearest unto divinity, the ancients erected an art of divination, wherein while they too widely expatiated in loose and inconsequent conjectures, Hippocrates wisely considered dreams" as presages of the alterations of the body and as hints for preserving health.

The remark about those who expatiated too widely is directed at Artemidorus, Achmet, *et al.* Indeed later in the work Browne states that, while some clearly ominous dreams admit of an "easie ... exposition", he cannot see why lettuce should stand for disease, eggs signify trouble, or blindness be a good sign. These interpretations, given in the oracular verses of Astrampsychos and Nicephoras, Browne leaves to our divination. Yet when he turns to analyzing the friend's dream, he indulges in similar mysteries.[75]

Browne's ambiguous pronouncements on the subject of interpretation reach a sort of climax of indeterminacy with a casual remark in a minor essay. He contends there that Scripture, being "hard", requires interpretation which, if rightly made, would yield information of importance to most sciences, including oneirocriticism:

Oneirocritical Diviners apprehend some hints of their knowledge, even from Divine Dreams; while they take notice of the Dreams of Joseph, Pharaoh, Nebuchadnezzar, and the Angels on Jacob's Ladder; and find, in Artemidorus and Achmetes, that Ladders signifie Travels, and the Scales thereof Preferment; and that Oxen Lean and Fat naturally denote Scarcity or Plenty, and the Success of Agriculture.[76]

Browne's point here is that the interpretations given in the Bible coincide with the significance assigned the same symbols by the pagan analysts. Is he then accepting as legitimate the methods of these "expatiators", or is he verifying their interpretation of the above symbols only – that is, where they accord with Scripture?

[75]   *Ibid.*, I, 174-75.
[76]   "Observations Upon Several Plants Mentioned in Scripture", in *Works*, V, 5.

Does his response to Hippocrates's method extend to the other pagans as well? There is no clear answer.

In any case, Browne's writings present us with an excellent example of the survival into the seventeenth century of dream theories old as history. The traditions of the supernatural dream engendered by god or demon; of the self-generated subjective dream; of the natural dream accounted for by waking thoughts or somatic disposition; of the interpretation of dreams for practical or medical purposes – all these traditions, traced in the course of this chapter, were being scrupulously examined by Sir Thomas Browne at the very time that Hobbes and the "new" philosophers were preparing to destroy them.

II

TYPICAL USES OF THE DREAM IN WESTERN LITERATURE

A. DREAM GENRES AND METAPHORS

Legend tells us that when Hecuba was about to give birth to Paris, she dreamed of a torch setting Troy on fire. The parents proceeded, in accordance with ancient mores, to expose the child. Surviving the ordeal, however, it brought about in later years the predestined disaster. Such a dream, which sums up an important event in history or fiction, can be matched with many others in antiquity. Epic, drama, history are full of dream-phantoms advising, prophesying, or demanding burial. A dream by a hero of his own death is a ready epical device to show the protagonist's foreknowledge and his bravery in the face of fate.[1] Indeed the dreams in virtually all ancient and medieval literature are concerned not with the past but with the future. These mantic dreams, by their very nature dramatic, lend a poetic validity to Casaubon's conjectured derivation (etymologically incorrect) of the word "dream" from the Greek *drama*.[2]

The dream is dramatic also if it has ontological validity, that is, if the experience it brings is, although transmitted through sleep, part of present reality. The belief in this "objective" dream was widespread in primitive culture. The dreamer's soul either

---

[1] This paragraph is based in part on A. Bouché-Leclerq, *Histoire de la divination dans l'antiquité* (Paris, 1879), I, 329-331. The story of Paris is widespread; an early version of it is in Ennius (*Remains of Old Latin*, trans. E. H. Warmington [London, 1935], I, 235-7).

[2] The OE word *swefn* (sleep, dream) was replaced by *dreme* (which once meant joy, music, noise) at the time of Chaucer (E. C. Ehrensperger, "Dreams Words in OE and ME", *PMLA,* XLVI [1931], pp. 80-88).

visited distant places and persons or passively observed the remote and esoteric brought into proximity by supernatural forces.[3] Sleep was merely a doorway into some stratum of reality not available to the waking man living in his little corner of the universe.

The simplest objective dream is the literal non-symbolic one. Its characteristic is that it does not refashion things into an allegory but presents existing reality. In the *Gilgamesh Epic,* for example, Enkidu, the close friend of the hero, is aroused from sleep in his last illness long enough to tell of his having been led to the palace of the Queen of Darkness. In this realm of darkness and dust, of priests working as petty servants and of kings without crowns, he was arrested by an emissary of the queen. At that climactic point, Enkidu awoke, drained of blood and in terror. This vision of Hell, besides being the main source for our knowledge of the Babylonian (and hence earliest) afterlife, is set down with expert craftsmanship; more than a vague dream, it depicts a kind of clairvoyance attained through sleep.[4]

Such a dream is literal, explicit, of unequivocal import. The majority of renowned dreams in literature, however, are symbolic or "allegoric". These are open to varying interpretations because of their frequently enigmatic symbolic language in which nothing is what it seems. The ancient Near Eastern works record such dreams only with their interpretations, without which they are "unopened letters".[5] A famous example in Greek Literature is Penlope's dream. She tells a seeming stranger, Odysseus in disguise, that she observed an eagle kill twenty geese; when she wept at the scene, the eagle returned to inform her that this was no mere dream but an omen of her husband's imminent return home. She then awoke. Her dream, while not furthering the plot, hints at the turbulent conclusion of the story.[6] Well-known

---

[3] On the objective dream see A. Leo Oppenheim, *The Interpretation of Dreams in the Ancient Near East* (Philadelphia, 1956), p. 226; and G. S. Brett, *A History of Psychology* (London, 1912), I, 10.

[4] *The Epic of Gilgamesh,* trans. N. K. Sandars (London, 1960), pp. 35, 89-90.

[5] On Near Eastern works see Oppenheim, p. 206.

[6] Homer, *Odyssey,* trans. S. Butler (New York, 1944), Bk. XIX, 11. 509-581; this dream is discussed by W. S. Messer, *The Dream in Homer and Greek Tragedy* (New York, 1918), pp. 31-2.

Biblical examples of symbolic visions are Joseph's two dreams. In one he beholds his brothers' sheaves bowing to his sheaf; in the other the sun, the moon, and eleven stars make obeisance to Joseph.[7] They exalt him over his brothers – who are quick to see this – and predict his future prominence in Egypt, of which his kin have no inkling. The dreams, moreover, motivate the brothers to get rid of the dreamer. Their treachery leads ironically to the fulfillment of the destiny foreshadowed in the dreams.

The literal and the symbolic, then, are two major types of dreams. This distinction is cut across by another: dreams can also be classified as either subjective or objective. While the subjective dream arises from the dreamer's own inner faculties, the objective is caused by some agency from without – whether the gods (who often appear in classical literature in the guise of living human beings) or ghosts of the dead. The nature of the objective dream can be seen in Xerxes's experience. After undergoing a divine-guidance dream, he places his skeptical advisor on his throne in his own regal clothes; the advisor has the same dream. Similarly in Pindar's story of the dream of Bellerophon, the hero is given a golden bridle; when he awakes, the bridle lies next to him.[8] In the objective dream, the apparition dreamed of seems to enter and alter the sleeper's consciousness or environment.

The dreams of antiquity and the Middle Ages fall into certain recognizable patterns. Although at times described as aural, they are usually visual. Objective dreams provide divine guidance or comfort; relay a warning, prohibition, promise, or cure; invite the dreamer to reform, convert, write, build, journey; or prophesy his renowned posterity. If the dream is important and unheeded, it recurs. Sometimes the fate predicted can be avoided by prudent action; on other occasions the dreams adumbrate the inevitable. Among common symbolic dreams is the pregnant mother's vision in which eminence is predicted for her child. Similarly, a dream

---

[7]   Gen. xxxvii. 5-11.

[8]   Herodotus, *Histories,* trans. G. Rawlinson (New York, 1942), vii. 12-19; Pindar, *Odes,* trans. Sir John Sandys (London, 1937), Olympian XIII, ll. 63-92.

informs one of a relative's death or of one's own imminent death. Ancient stories of the procreation of a prominent person-to-be are usually associated with the dream experience, as are the construction of famous buildings and cities, the inception of literary or artistic works.[9]

Dreams could be solicited by various means. Moreover, as a result of the widespread belief in the validity of the dream, the experience was often feigned by a person desiring to effect something.[10] Finally, the dream was utilized as a figure of speech. The transferred sense of the word normally indicates any kind of thinking, daydreaming, or procrastinating. A simile or metaphor based on the dream experience itself delineates a quality in some other thing, a quality which the dream conspicuously possesses. In this manner it has been used as a figure for an abrupt cessation; a foul thing; a lie; a familiar thing; an intimate, secret thing; the after-life; the chaotic or mad; the elusive and insubstantial; the incredible; feebleness or paralysis; transience; and extreme joy. By far the most widespread figurative use of the dream is as an image of something unreal, especially as something symbolic of the human condition beside the greater reality of eternity. In the oldest extant writings of man, the pleasures of life – and indeed all earthly affairs – are likened to a dream. Homer having compared something insubstantial to a shadow or a dream, Pindar goes on to say in a famous line: "Creatures of a day, what is any one? What is he not? Man is but a dream of a shadow."[11] One of the great lyric statements of this outlook is Walther von der Vogelweide's famous elegiac swan song, "Owê war sint verswunden alliu mîniu jâr!/ist mir mîn leben getroumet? oder is ez wâr?" Finding himself old, he wonders whether his life has been real or only a dream. Although he feels awake now, everything

---

[9] For the dream of a pregnant mother see, e.g., Herodotus vi. 131; the dream of one's own imminent death: Plutarch, trans. "J. Dryden" (New York, n.d.), *Alcibiades* xxxix; the dream of the procreation of a great man: Plutarch, *Alexander* ii; the dream of artistic inspiration: Callimachus, *Fragments*, trans. C. A. Trypanis (London, 1958), p. 2.

[10] See, e.g., II Macc. xv. 11-17; and Lucian, *Works*, trans. A. M. Harmon and K. Kilburn (London, 1913-1961), *Alexander* xlix.

[11] Pindar, Pythian VIII, 11. 92-96.

seems altered. The world he knew as a child has grown strange; the lovely days are fled, the trees cut down, the friends remote.[12] Some four hundred years later, Calderón de la Barca constructed an entire play on the theme of the dream-like quality of life: *Life is a Dream.*[13]

B. VISION WORKS: THE HEURISTIC DREAM

I turn now to some typical uses of the dream in Western literature. First to be examined is the eschatological dream as well as the related genre of extended narrative visions. Then I will discuss the love dream prominent in the lyric, and the mantic dream common in drama and history. Dreams embedded in fictional narrative, on the other hand, have varied uses, the survey of which concludes this chapter.

The tradition of eschatological dreams begins with Enkidu's dream in *Gilgamesh* of the afterworld. Among classical writers, Cicero alleges that such a dream occurred to Scipio Aemilianus, the destroyer of Carthage and grandson of the conqueror of Hannibal. The story is actually Cicero's fabrication modelled on Plato's vision of Er. In the *Republic,* Socrates tells of the soldier who died in battle and returned to life after a twelve-day visit to the other world, where he saw the cosmos, the spheres, and the rewards and punishments being administered to souls. Socrates's point is that, although virtue is its own reward, there are other gains as well in store for the good man.[14] Borrowing the story for his own purposes, Cicero changes the special vision to a normal objective dream, in which the conqueror of Hannibal appears to his grandson and predicts his future great career. Scipio Africanus then explains the structure of the universe, the music of the spheres, the vanity of earthly fame, the immortality of the soul, the true glory of virtue and of comtemplation. Answering the dreamer's questions as to the next world, he imbues him with a sense of

---

12   *Spruche. Lieder. Der Leich,* ed. P. Stapf (Berlin, 1955), p. 183.
13   Trans. W. Colford (New York, 1958).
14   Plato, *Dialogues,* trans. B. Jowett (New York, 1937), I, 870-79.

responsibility to his station in life. Cicero's innovation lies here, for, as one scholar has remarked, even a work which directs the mind away from the immediate things of this world closes with a Roman admonition that the "best tasks are those undertaken in defense of one's native land". However, to Macrobius – who thinks that Cicero adopted the dream frame because Plato's version was ridiculed for being a fable – Cicero's piece conveys all the basic teachings of the three branches of philosophy: moral, physical, rational.[15]

In time the genre became Christianized. Bede, for example, tells of a cleric, Fursa, who dreamed of Hell and Heaven.[16] The most refined and sophisticated of many Christian versions occurs in Tasso's *Jerusalem Delivered*.[17] At the same time, when the eschatological dream is enlarged in scope and detail, as in the *Vision of Tungdale*, it becomes a full-scale "vision" work. In this

[15] Macrobius, *Commentary on the Dream of Scipio*, trans. W. H. Stahl (New York, 1952), pp. 69-77, 83, 246; the quotation is from Moses Hadas, *A History of Latin Literature* (New York, 1952), p. 127.

[16] Bede, *Works*, trans. J. E. King (London, 1930), III, xix.

[17] A celestial dream is experienced by the Christian champion, Godfrey, in time of severe stress. The vision places him on a point of vantage from which to observe the stars, harmonies, vast spheres, golden fires. We recognize here the cosmic scope of Scipio's dream. And as in that famous story, a guide appears to Godfrey: his dead comrade in arms, Hugo of Vermandois. They try thrice in vain to embrace, in the venerable epic manner. Informing Godfrey that a place here awaits him, Hugo takes him on a tour of the heavenly kingdom. At Hugo's behest, Godfrey looks down to the small speck that is the earth – as did Dante guided by Beatrice – and feels a *contemptus mundi*, wondering at man's greed to possess such a trifle. Hugo then imparts advice, moral and political. The latter kind includes a mandate to recall and forgive Rinaldo, for it is God's wish that Godfrey should plan and Rinaldo execute. Neither can function without the other. Their blood, moreover, will be mixed – here begins the prophecy of posterity – in a great lineage of heroes. Hugo disappears as Godfrey awakens with wonder and joy, ready to undertake the recall of his foremost knight. Thus in one colorful objective dream inserted at a crucial point are fused several themes: the hero's vision of eternity; the contrast between the wonders of heaven and the pettiness of man on earth; the prophecy of posterity; the advice of immediate importance for continuing the story line, reaching the denouement, and imparting moral significance. Tasso here draws on virtually everything classical and medieval in the tradition of the hero's divine-guidance, eschatological dream (*Jerusalem Delivered*, trans. E. Fairfax, ed. H. Morley [London, 1890], pp. 290-94).

genre the dream is used as a mere frame within which to set an extended description or story, or to develop a philosophical, political, or satirical critique. Psychological realism is ignored. Furthermore, the dream is heuristic rather than mantic: it helps one to learn something of the eternal instead of foretelling the future.

The tradition of the dream vision has roots in antiquity. Although Hesiod's *Theogony* begins with a waking vision of the Muses, his device of a personal prelude is turned by Callimachus into a dream wherein the Muses instruct him in mythology. A Christian analogue to such a work is the Anglo Saxon "Dream of the Rood", in which the Cross relates to the dreamer the story of the Passion and urges him to spread the good news.[18]

The genre of dream visions flourished in the Middle Ages; such works as *Pearl* and *Tungdale* are merely two well-known examples out of many. Boethius's *Consolations of Philosophy* and Dante's *Commedia* may be regarded as vast waking visions of similar import, while *Piers Plowman,* composed of numerous dreams, is a vision work in which eschatology is displaced by allegorical satire of contemporary moral and political evils. The vision frame is used also in works dealing entirely with secular matters. Thus the *Roman de la Rose* is a dream, experienced by a lover, in which the allegorical personifications depict the states of mind encountered and the experiences undergone during the courtship of a beloved. Even so scientific a work as Oresme's *De commensurabilitate* features a debate between Arithmetic and Geometry overheard in a dream.[19]

The unexpressed reasoning behind this vision convention seems to be that to have the allegorical personifications – which are a way of rendering visible the invisible movements of faculties and desires – disport and declaim is an unreality which only the dream experience can justify. The medieval poet thereby implies that if we had sufficient insight this is what we would see while awake;

---

[18]   Hesiod, trans. R. Lattimore (Ann Arbor, 1959), 11. 1 ff.; Callimachus, p. 2; "The Dream of the Rood" in *Anglo Saxon Poetry*, trans. R. K. Gordon (London, 1926), pp. 261-65.
[19]   For Oresme see A. H. Thorndike, *A History of Magic and Experimental Science* (New York, 1923-1958), III, 405.

instead we attain the insight in sleep when the spirit is freed from the flesh. Though Freud regards sleep as the liberator of the irrational, the medieval poet, on the contrary, believes that it sometimes cooperates with the rational. As Langland puts it, "Reason had ruth on me and rocked me to slumber"; then he saw "as by sorcery" a creature and – the allegory begins.[20]

A frequent utilizer of the dream frame is Chaucer in his early works, influenced by the *Roman de la Rose* and its large progeny in France. In the Prologue to the *Legend of Good Women*, the persona, after walking through the springtime meadows, goes to sleep in an arbor and dreams of roaming again in the fields; there he meets Love, whose rebuke leads him, when awakened, to tell tales of good women.[21] The dream in this way accounts for the creation of the work. In other poems Chaucer transcends the trite mechanism of falling asleep at the beginning of the work and awakening at the end – a device designed to get the character into the medieval fairyland of personified abstractions. He alters the conventional to achieve verisimilitude, the real unreality of dreams.[22]

In the *Book of the Duchess,* for example, the persona declares himself ill and weary – a cause of dreams, according to contemporary theory – yet the "I" within the dream is active. After telling us of his sleeplessness and his reading of Ovid in bed, the persona falls asleep and dreams that he casually runs into the Emperor Octavian hunting. Nothing is said of the site or circumstances, nor is any wonder expressed. A horse and puppy appear, then vanish without further reference to them. He meets a bereaved husband – and quite properly so, because he has been reading of a similar bereavement in Ovid. The intrusion of reality, when the dreamer finds out the truth of the lady's death and when the clock strikes, marks the moment of awaking. So profound was the dream that the dreamer has forgotten his own woes. We have, then, in the midst of the clichés and stage props

20 William Langland, *The Vision of Piers Plowman,* trans. H. W. Wells (New York, 1945), p. 192.
21 Geoffrey Chaucer, *Works,* ed. F. N. Robinson (Boston, Second Ed., 1957), pp. 485 ff.
22 The genre is discussed by G. L. Kittredge, *Chaucer and His Poetry* (New York, 1915), pp. 22, 38, 58, 60, 66-71, 74-76.

of the tradition, a man in bed experiencing a dream that refracts, if not reflects, waking thoughts – a vivid life-like dream.[23]

A famous Renaissance vision is the *Dream of Poliphilus,* a fifteenth-century Italian work which, as the subtitle of the partial Elizabethan translation says, deals with "the combat of love in a dream, showing human things are a dream". After a restless night in bed, an unrequited lover falls asleep and dreams he is lost in a wild, thick wood. He finally rests wearily under a tree and dreams of being in a beautiful valley with large edifices. In this dream-within-a-dream, he wanders through a fantastic landscape of statuary, art works, and buildings in many architectural styles. These are described at length and illustrated with lavish woodcuts. Eventually he comes to a palace of ladies, takes part in Temple of Venus' ceremonies, and by the end of Book I joins his beloved, Polia.

The woodcuts, besides making this something of a cartoonstrip romance, are revelatory of the late fifteenth-century love of classical antiquity. The hero is more in love with Roman architecture and ornaments than with Polia; the real dream in the book is a monk's insatiate desire for material loveliness, for a feast of knowledge, art, language, love. A product of the Renaissance rediscovery of the classical past, this work reveals how new content was being poured into old literary forms.[24]

C. LYRIC AND ROMANCE: THE LOVE DREAM

Although the early Greek lyric contains a few references to the dreams of personages in the Troy story, it is not until Sappho

---

[23]   Chaucer, pp. 267-68; this paragraph is based on J. R. Kreuzer, "Dreams in the *Book of the Duchess"*, *PMLA* (1951), pp. 543-47. The *Parliament of Foules* (pp. 310 ff.) and the *House of Fame* (pp. 281 ff.) are likewise dream-vision works; in fact, one scholar has gone so far as to conjecture that Chaucer's masterpiece, *The Canterbury Tales,* may have grown out of the dream-vision tradition (J. V. Cunningham, "The Literary Tradition of the Prologue of the *Canterbury Tales"*, *MP* [1952], pp. 174-76, 179-180).
[24]   F. Colonna, *The Strife of Love in a Dream,* trans. anon., ed. A. Lang (London, 1890).

that we find the first traces of a dream genre late to develop but destined to achieve wide currency: the love dream. Such visions, like the other early ones in epic, are objective and closely related to the actions of the gods. Thus one poem is a prayer to Hera to set in a dream beside the poetess in bed a beautiful person; another begins, "I dreamt that I talked with the Cyprus-born."[25]

Absent from classical epic, drama, and history, the love dream began to proliferate in the lyrics of Hellenistic Greece. In the *Anacreontea* we read that the swallow's sounds destroy the poet's sweet dream of his beloved; we meet for the first time anecdotes of Cupid, either appearing in a dream or interrupting a love dream.[26] In the *Greek Anthology* we hear of the lover who, after spending a sleepless night, urges the birds to leave so that he can sleep and dream of his beloved in his arms; or of the lover who dreams that a high-priced courtesan of the city lies with him all night; whose dream of enjoying his lady is interrupted by Eros, jealous even in visions and chasing away sleep and bliss; who dreams of a yearning for, or possession of, boys.[27] The burden of all these poems is that sleep, which brings to most people release from toil and cares, can be to the lover either an exacerbation of love-longing or a pander for the imagination. The love dream itself is neither heuristic[28] nor mantic – although the awakened dreamer would like it to be so – but simply a means of depicting the intensity of the lover's feelings, of rendering homage to the lady's physical attractiveness, and of obtaining through fantasy what is lacking in reality.

In Roman poetry the love-dream, used as the subject of an extended poem, came to artistic flower.[29] The best of Propertius's

---

[25]   *Lyra* Graeca, trans. J. M. Edmonds (Londen, 1928), Sappho # 40, 85, 118, 123.

[26]   *Anacreontea,* trans. J. M. Edmonds (London, 1931), poems 10, 30, 34.

[27]   *The Greek Anthology,* trans. W. R. Paton (London, 1916), I, 247-251; IV, 343-345.

[28]   To be sure, the Stoics, as we saw in Chapter One, believed that erotic and incestuous dreams teach us something about the state of our souls. But the love poets, no paragons of Stoicism, used such dreams in their poetry for other than heuristic purposes.

[29]   For an example see Tibullus, *Works,* trans. W. K. Kelly (London, 1927), III, iv.

love-dream references concern specters in objective visions. In one poem, the dead daughter of Scipio urges her husband not to mourn her before their children but to wait for nighttime when her features will appear in his dreams and he will talk to her as though she could answer. In another elegy the recently buried Cynthia appears, charred and tarnished, at her sleeping lover's bed. Scolding him for his indifference to her passing away and urging him to take care of her affairs, she tells of Hades and of famous chaste and adulterous women who confess their life stories there. With the warning that he will soon join her, she vanishes from between his arms.[30] This moving poem was germinal; we sense here already the lover's visions of Beatrice or Laura after death, the flavor of some of Ronsard's best lyrics, and much else in the Renaissance.

Another tenderly handled love-dream, in Ovid, reveals the plight of young Biblis, enamored of her brother. Suppressing her desires during the day, she beholds in sleep their consummation. When awakened, she wishes the dreams to return again because in them there are no witnesses and she does not have to be on her guard. Yet she wonders what they mean and whether she really wants them realized. While she might marvel at the relation of dream to reality, we can see that this love dream serves to crystallize in her innocent mind the goal of her untutored passion.[31]

The rise of the love lyric in twelfth- and thirteenth-century Europe, after a thousand year lapse from its currency in late Greek literature, naturally gave renewed life to the love dream, at the same time that this kind of dream was making its appearance in Arthurian romance. The dream is usually so pleasant that when the lover awakens he weeps. In fact the awakening in a dream poem involves the same joy and pain found in the lyric of morning parting, the *alba*. Poems by Friedrich von Hausen, Hartmann von Aue, and Giraut de Borneil adhere to this love-

---

[30]   *Works,* trans. J. S. Philimore (Oxford, 1906), II, xxvi; IV, vii, xi.
[31]   *Metamorphoses,* trans. R. Humphries (New York, 1955), IX, 470-500. The love dream functions in the same way in Longus's *Daphnis and Chloe,* trans. G. Thornley (London, 1916), II, 10-11.

dream convention,[32] which is somewhat modified in the most famous of such lyrics, Heinrich von Morungen's "Mirst geschên": Love brings the poet's beloved to him in a dream; as he grows ecstatic at sight of her, he notices that her mouth is slightly disturbed and ashy pale. He falls into a new sorrow and compares his fate to that of Narcissus.

The burden of this poem may be that the dream image of the beloved becomes a mirror in which the lover sees himself; that is, although she appears to have enchanted him, he has really enchanted himself by surrendering to his own emotions and to the easeful death of courtly love, *Minne*. Or perhaps the point is that the poet can contemplate the lady's ideal beauty and virtues only in the imagination; perfection appears exclusively in a dream and is a dream – insubstantial, deceiving, unrealizable. Yet even in the dream his joy is flawed by her paleness and disturbed mouth. Whatever its exact meaning, the poem is a triumph because of the reverberation of its clear images – the mirror, the dream lady, the Narcissus figure – in harmony with the eery suggestiveness of the dream and its nebulous connection to reality. Since we are not told why she is disturbed, the final impression is one of a precise imprecision suitable to dreams.[33]

Among early Renaissance poets, Petrarch, in spite of expressed distrust of dreams,[34] has several love-dream lyrics. He experiences a dream, for instance, of Laura, desperately ill, urging him not to despair; of her angelic face, which often consoled him in his dreams when she was distant, informing him that he will never see her again. In the poems after the death of Laura, the dream

---

[32] Friedrich and Hartmann are in *Medieval German Lyrics,* ed. and trans. M. Richey (London, 1958), pp. 40, 59; Giraut is in *Anthologie des Troubadors,* ed. and trans. J. Anglade (Paris, 1927), pp. 72-81.

[33] Included in *Deutsche Lyrik des Mittelalters,* ed. and trans. Max Wehrli (Zurich, 1955), pp. 147, 533, 577. See also two fine dream poems by the master of medieval lyrists, Walther von der Vogelweide; containing dreams free of any mantic or psychological significance, these poems savor of a fresh, gentle, Heine-like irony (Walther, pp. 134, 150).

Cf. also, in Chaucer's incomplete translation of the *Roman de la Rose,* a passage which presents the paradigm of the love-dream lyric (*Works,* p. 589).

[34] Quoted in J. H. Robinson, *Petrarch* (New York, 1901), pp. 43-46.

experiences become more frequent and serve as a bridge between this world and the next. She appears to be more beautiful now; she fondles him; her presence makes his grief bearable until the dawn abruptly ends the dream. In one of these visions, his daring to confess his passion to her phantom causes her to weep in pity. He weeps as well, then suddenly awakens.[35] These poems, owing much to the tradition of the previous two centuries, became in turn immensely influential on the love-dream lyrics of the later European Renaissance.

D. DRAMA AND HISTORY: THE OMINOUS MANTIC DREAM

The dreams in Greek tragedy – mainly in Aeschylus – derive, like much else, from the epic tradition rather than from life. There are few dreams in the myths; the dramatists felt free to add to them under the influence of the epics. Penelope's dream of the geese, the one symbolic vision in Homer, was seminal for Greek drama (and, in fact, for Hellenistic Greek and Imperial Roman epic), in which most dreams were symbolic and experienced by women. The circumstances of the drama, however, tended to alter some traits of the dream. Thus the source of the experience, clearly shown in the epic to be the gods, often went unmarked in the play.[36]

Such is the case with the examples in Aeschylus, a master craftsman in the use of this material. The circumstances following Atossa's ominous symbolic dream of Xerxes' disaster in "The Persians", for instance, make it one of the impressive events in literature. On awakening, she undertakes rites of purification but is distracted by the portentous behavior of a falcon and eagle. Her dream, apparently Aeschylus's happy invention, motivates the appearance of Darius's ghost and dominates the economy of the play as no dream does that of the Greek epic.

---

[35] *Sonnets*, trans. J. Auslander (New York, 1932), # 33, 190, 250, 282, 356.
[36] This paragraph is based on Messer, pp. 28, 33, 57-59, 65, 69, 85.

When news comes of Xerxes' actual defeat – the fulfillment of the dream – Atossa still has not undertaken the purification rites. With a fine determination, she insists on doing so in any case.[37]

The most completely integrated dream in a Greek literary work is Clytemnestra's in "The Libation Bearers". As the play opens, the chorus, whom she has sent out with a libation to avert the ill omen, is a living manifestation of the dream terror which has affected her. They suppose her to be haunted by Agamemnon. Only gradually is the dream-content – that she gave birth to a snake which wounded the breast she tendered it – revealed to the audience and to Orestes. The play then reverberates with this image. His determination fortified by the vision, Orestes begins to identify himself with the serpent. When he prepares to kill his mother, she says with unconscious irony:

> Oh take pity, child, before this breast
> Where many a time, a drowsing baby, you would feed
> And with soft gums sucked in the milk that made you strong.

Her words falling on deaf ears, she suddenly sees the connection between them and her dream: "You are the snake I gave birth to, and I gave the breast." Lest this remark be only a figure of speech, Orestes applies it specifically to the dream: "Indeed the terror of your dreams saw things to come/Clearly."[38]

Thus the vision, after setting the machinery of the play going, is referred to darkly at crucial moments, especially at the climax. That it is but gradually revealed, interpreted, and realized heightens the suspense and overshadows the play's action. A variation on the mother's mantic dream of her child (except that she dreams it long after the child's birth), it bristles with ironies. The person to interpret it – in the very moment of its realization – is her own child as well as its murderous fulfiller. The chorus, sent to avert the dream omen, witnesses instead its fulfillment.[39]

Exciting as this dream is, an even bolder stroke is found in

[37] Aeschylus, *Tragedies,* trans. D. Grene and R. Lattimore (New York, n.d.), "The Persians," 11. 176-231, 517-526.
[38] "The Libation Bearers", 11. 32-46, 514-550, 896-98, 928-930.
[39] This analysis is based on Messer, pp. 70-73.

"The Eumenides". There the Furies dream on the stage, and the ghost of Clytemnestra – the substance of half the dream – appears for all to see. Objective and subjective elements freely mingle. The Furies' "natural" subjective dream of pursuing Orestes as they rest from that task is encroached upon by the objective dream of the wraith that rebukes them for letting him get away. The ghost's presence and demands owe much to Patroclus's request of Achilles; this is, in fact, the only non-symbolic dream in Greek tragedy. Structurally the dream propels the plot and signalizes the important change in Orestes's life. He is emerging from his conscience-stricken stupor and expiation into an evaluation of his crime, into trial and judgment. His mother's wraith attempts to stop the change, but the tormented dead cannot affect the redemption of the living.[40] Thus we see that the dreams in the drama have an ominous, prophetic quality unlike the heuristic function of the eschatological dreams and of the extended dream-visions, or the erotic and psychological function of the love-lyric dreams.

Writing during the age of Greek tragedy, Herodotus presents, amid his large collection of dreamlore, several stories that reflect themes of the drama. To the very beginning of his work, he affixes two dreams which sound a basic leitmotif: the instability of human happiness and the inevitability of man's fate. In one story, Croesus condemns Solon because the Athenian has been unwilling to call the king happy until he has witnessed his end. Croesus soon thereafter dreams that his one healthy son, Atys, will be killed by a spear. Frightened, he refuses to let the son go to the wars and removes all weapons from the palace. Once, however, he reluctantly allows Atys to join in the hunt for a loose boar. Unfortunately Atys's guard Adrastus, who was given refuge at Croesus's court after killing someone by accident, throws a spear which misses the boar and slays the prince. Thus the dream prophecy fulfills itself in spite of all the preventive measures. The simple literalism of Atys – who protested that it would be safe for him to hunt the boar since the dream

---

40   "Eumenides", II. 94-140; see Messer's analysis, pp. 74-77.

specified a spear rather than a boar's tusk – is exposed: man does not know what gods and dreams intend. That Adrastus was appointed to protect the very man whom he would kill, as well as the fact that he was already tainted with accidental manslaughter, adds to the irony. Most important of all, Croesus comes thereby to understand the wisdom of Solon's teaching. Herodotus has here used the dream to construct a miniature Greek tragedy.[41]

The intimations of Fate in Greek tragedy – specifically *Oedipus* – are even clearer in Herodotus's story of a baby exposed by a king because of an ominous dream. Saved by someone's pity, the child grows up to become Cyrus the Great. In another story, Cambyses kills his brother Smerdis because of a dream, only to discover that the culprit who will undo him is a pretender assuming the name of Smerdis. Moreover, Cambyses's madness is dated from the time of that dream. Here we run into an important use of the dream in ancient culture: to account for the unknown. When a man's behavior changed withouth any external visible reason, the irrational could be domesticated and understood – for want of an elaborate and sophisticated psychology – by referring the change to a dream. This reasoning is rendered explicit in Herodotus's story of Xerxes; he took Athens and planned to burn it but on the following day was lenient to the Greeks, perhaps because "he had had a dream which bade him give this order". Similarly, when an Ethiopian ruler of Egypt voluntarily stepped down from his throne or when a Persian general resettled a conquered land, the motivation for such apparently strange actions was found by Herodotus solely in dreams, even though in actuality complex economic and political pressures might have played a role. The ancient reader was apparently satisfied with such an explanation.[42]

---

[41]   Herodotus i. 33-45.
[42]   *Ibid.*, i. 107-111; iii, 30, 64; viii. 54; ii. 139, 152; iii, 149.

E. NARRATIVE WORKS: CELESTIAL, INFERNAL, AND
INTERRELATED DREAMS

While dreams have many functions in long narrative works, the kinds we have looked at so far – heuristic, erotic, ominous and mantic – do not generally appear in classical epic. We find instead dreams of practical guidance and monition, whether caused by the gods – friendly or hostile to the dreamer – by dream-*daimones* or by ghosts of the dead. Such experiences, occurring usually to a major character, motivate his actions, account for irrational decisions, or create an atmosphere of suspense and awe. Near the end of the *Iliad*, for instance, Achilles dreams that the recently slain Patroclus entreats him to bury the dead body – so that Patroclus' spirit may be admitted to the netherworld – and warns that Achilles too will soon die. The dreamer attempts to embrace the apparition but awakens as it vanishes. When fully conscious, he accepts the validity of the dream as containing an objective wraith endowed with prophetic power. This dream of a dead person, the first of many in European literature, spans the barriers separating life and death – in accordance with primitive beliefs about the dream – and brings vital information to the hero.[43] Many important dreams in the *Aeneid* are such visions of wraiths.

More prevalent in ancient literature is the celestial dream. The apparition, usually supernaturally tall and handsome, stands at the head of the sleeper whom it addresses by name. In the Greek epic the objective reality of the dream is enhanced by indications of the god's actually entering and leaving the room.[44] In the *Aeneid,* the gods as well as the wraiths guide the hero by means of dreams. Mercury's arousing Aeneas to action provides the hero with a motivation for an abrupt departure from Dido that would have seemed cold and unchivalrous if undertaken on his own initiative. Later on, when Latinus solicits divine guidance, he is told in his dream not to marry his daughter to Turnus. The sub-

[43]   *The Iliad,* trans. S. Butler (New York, 1942), xxiii. 62-107; this dream is discussed by Messer, pp. 12-19.
[44]   On objective divine dreams, see Oppenheim, pp. 186-191.

sequent important dream prophecy of the mixing of Trojan and Latin races causes Latinus to give Lavinia to Aeneas rather than to do battle with the invading people.[45]

Of perhaps greater interest for its impact on later literature is the objective dream caused by an evil supernatural power or a god antagonistic to the hero. The prototype is the controversial dream in the second book of the *Iliad*. Zeus, acceding to Thetis's request to honor the sulking Achilles by having the Greeks routed,

---

[45] Virgil, *Aeneid*, trans. L. Hart and V. R. Osborn (New York, 1882), iv. 554-572; vii. 81-101; this dream is discussed by H. R. Steiner, *Der Traum in der Aeneis* (Berne, 1952), pp. 53, 59-60.

At the climax of Apuleius's *Golden Ass*, Lucius, ready for deliverance from his ass-hood, experiences a series of objective visions of the beautiful goddess Isis and of the supreme god Osiris. Besides forewarning and guiding, this sequence of dreams is a sign of favor towards a human soul gravitating closer to the Eternal after having undergone purifying suffering as an ass. Similar to the experiences of many later mystics and saints, in associating the numinous dream with the morally purified state of the dreamer, this sequence brings us closer to the Christian dream (trans. R. Graves [New York, 1951], pp. 263-287).

The *raison d'etre* for the dreams in Homer and Virgil – a divine interest in man's activities – existed in the Middle Ages with even greater force. If reality indeed lay elsewhere than in this vale of tears, as it probably never fully did for most pagans, the dream was a quick way of getting there while one was still moored in the flesh. It was a more intense existence to the medieval poet; it offered a way beyond the "dark glass". Hence we find in Eusebius's *Ecclesiastical History*, Gregory of Tours's *History of the Franks*, and particularly Jacobus de Voragine's *Golden Legend* vast collections of dreams. A certain medieval writer spoke of virtuous clerics being often consoled towards the end of their lives by visions of the Lord and angels. Jacobus's book is in effect "all about" that very fact. After a short sketch of each saint's life and death comes a series of tales of his dreams and, especially, his appearance in others' visions.

Furthermore, in a dream related by Gregory of Tours we see something familiar. An abbot whose one fault has been to rule by entreaty instead of fear is told one night in a symbolic dream that those remiss in governing their flocks will be punished. The abbot awakens and becomes stricter from then on (*History of the Franks*, trans. O. M. Dalton [Oxford, 1927], IV, 32). Have we not here the old attempt to account with a dream – in lieu of a more exact theory of the personality – for an inexplicable change of character? Similarly, while the pagan recalled the mantic dream by the pregnant mother of a warrior son, the Christian hallowed the dream of the mother of the saint. The pagan slept in the temple to obtain a dream cure; the medieval man slept at a saint's shrine. The other genres were Christianized in like ways.

sends a false dream that urges Agamemnon to take Troy with a prompt attack. The false dream relays the message to the sleeping king in the form of Nestor, whose counsel is most valued. After the king awakens and informs his council of the dream, the real Nestor advises that, since Agamemnon is the greatest among them, the vision must be authentic. The Greeks proceed confidently to battle but are beaten.

This dream is, first of all, entirely objective. The figure stands above the head of the dreamer and addresses him as would a god. Although not referred to again later on, the dream ultimately plays a role in Agamemnon's eventual reconciliation with Achilles. Yet, although sent by Zeus, it is false; it beguiles both the ruler and his foremost counsellor and leads to a disaster. The ancient world was understandably troubled by this – especially later antiquity, which tended to attribute moral qualities to Zeus. Hence Plato, censuring Homer for his slander of the gods, used this incident as sufficient reason for barring poets from the Republic.[46]

In Virgil's version of this kind of dream, the Fury Alecto appears to Turnus, the antagonist of the epic, and rouses him to action. The dialogue within the dream, modelled on Penelope's geese dream, heightens its dramatic impact. As she reveals the new wedding arrangements and advances with snakes and torches, he awakens calling madly for arms. The rage transmitted from the Fury to Turnus – a graphic way of indicating inspiration or possession – sets the stage for the martial last section of the *Aeneid* and looks forward to Turnus's death in the bloody wars to come.[47] We have here a clear change in the character of the deceptive dream: although both Homer's and Virgil's incite the warrior into battles ultimately detrimental to his own cause, the dream in the Greek epic springs from the whim of Zeus, in the Latin work from the hatred of Juno. While in Homer Juno is

---

[46]   *Iliad* ii. 1-83; Plato II, 647. Plato, however, accepts the falsity of the dream. Later writers resort to sophistry in order to save the reputation of both Zeus and Homer; see Synesius, *Essays and Hymns,* trans. A. Fitzgerald (London, 1930), p. 347; and Macrobius, pp. 91, 118. The dream is analyzed by Messer, pp. 3-8.

[47]   *Aeneid* vii. 413-461; the dream is analyzed by Steiner, pp. 63-66.

merely one goddess with interests which happen to run counter to those of Zeus and Athena, her behavior in Virgil constitutes almost a dissent from some sort of cosmic order. The dream she generates in Turnus, dispatched through the agency of a Fury, approximates therefore the infernal or diabolic visions of later literature.

Under the Christian dispensation, moreover, the cosmic order is no longer a sensitive pagan's velleity but a widely shared certitude. "Demonic" dreams therefore become infernal, diabolic – part of the Devil's grand plan to foil God and the good. Christian literature is, of course, filled with such dreams. In Tasso's *Jerusalem Delivered,* for instance, the infernal Alecto appears to Argillan, a knight in Godfrey's crusade army, to propel him into a vindictive rage. The spirit falsely asserts that a headless body recently discoverd is that of Rinaldo, whose absense, caused by the wiles of Armida the witch, created unrest in the Christian camp. Desiring to avenge Rinaldo's death with the blood of Godfrey, Argillan awakens, arms, and rushes out to harangue the troops. With Alecto's help, the mutiny spreads to the camps of the Swiss and English.[48] Tasso uses the dream here in the primitive manner of accounting for the irrational, namely that Christian knights should turn against their pious leader. What has been altered, however, is the source of the dream. Instead of a goddess who, although against the hero for some previous slight, is neither more nor less morally delinquent than the gods favoring the hero, Tasso uses infernal creatures that deliberately set themselves against the whole moral order. If Virgil is the source of this dream, it is a Virgil fortified by centuries of Christian literature. From here it is but a short step to Eve's dream in *Paradise Lost.*[49]

---

[48] Tasso, pp. 189-191.

[49] The intermediary between Tasso and Milton, Spenser, uses the infernal dream in a way peculiar to his allegory. Archimago is intent on separating the Red Cross Knight, in quest of holiness, from Una. He therefore orders a spirit to instill into the knight a dream obtained from Morpheus. It is a lascivious vision, in which the chaste Una, who lies nearby, makes advances to the knight and enters his bed. Afraid of doing something wrong – his conscience not wholly extinguished by sleep – the knight awakens with a start. To make sure of his plot, Archimago manipulates the environment as well; he turns one of his other servant spirits into a "false Una",

As the many examples of supernatural dreams may suggest, the natural "realistic" dream makes its appearance in epic and romance works only fitfully. In Book XX of the *Odyssey*, Penelope mentions in prayer that while other persons are free from troubles at least in sleep, she herself is haunted even in dreams. During the past night Odysseus seemed to be lying next to her, looking as he had before leaving. Thinking him really present, she was happy.[50] Here we have one of the earliest examples of a subjective natural dream reflecting waking sorrow or presenting a wish-fulfillment: a vision caused by human emotions rather than gods. The tenderness of the scene is heightened by the dramatic irony of Odysseus's actual presence in the house.

The Virgilian version of this kind of dream is again an im-

---

who now makes advances to the awakened knight. The hero sends her away, then lies down wondering at the change in the chaste Una. Sleep soon returns, with the loose dreams again in its train. Aware that he is unsuccessful, however, Archimago finally abandons the knight to an untroubled sleep (*Works*, ed. R. E. Neil Dodge [Boston, 1908], *The Faerie Queene*, Bk. I, Canto i, st. 46-55).

This vision is interesting for several reasons. A male erotic dream, its content is "realistic". Yet placed in the frame of the traditional objective dream with external causes, it is in fact a dream sent by infernal creatures. Since we are dealing with allegory, moreover, Archimago and his tricks function also as a representation of those evil impulses *within* the soul which hinder the Christian voyage to Holiness. The dream is consequently both objective and subjective. Or, to take another approach, the dream-content resembles Arthur's dream of Gloriana – except for the licentiousness – the latter vision prompting the central knight of the allegory to seek the Queen of Fairyland (III, ii, 22-29). This repetition is part of Spenser's insight into the nature of moderation, his understanding that good and bad are often a matter of degree. Arthur's dream adumbrates the right kind of love, the kind that arouses a man, a knight, and a Christian to a nobler life. Without causing harm, it incites the proper instincts and prophesies a happy fulfillment. On the other hand, the Red Cross Knight's dream, itself a masquerade and misrepresentation, is a study in excess and lust. It is created by Hypocrisy to separate Truth from the soul in quest of Holiness, that is, to instill false beliefs about Truth into the soul, which can never be holy so long as it is misinformed, in the widest sense of the word. Arthur's dream is in the best of the courtly love tradition, the Red Cross Knight's a debasement of it. (Technically, this dream brings us closer to Eve's in *Paradise Lost*, in that the diabolic spirit causing it does not appear in its own guise in the dream itself.)

[50] *Odyssey* xx. 61-90.

provement. The love passion pervading Book IV produces in Dido at the time of Aeneas's departure a fine vision: she sees herself left all alone in a desert on a long journey seeking her Tyrians, like Pentheus or Orestes pursued by the Furies. In this vision there are no supernatural forces, no gods or dead souls. A dream of anxiety – the only subjective, natural one in Virgil – it has a dream symbol of timeless significance, far superior in atmospheric effect to the one symbolic dream in Homer. Without decisive meaning, it yet articulates her mood and fortifies her resolution to die; the allusion to Orestes and the Furies enhances her tragic role. The vision speaks in its own language, the haunting surrealist language of man's dreams.[51]

Lastly we turn to the sophisticated utilization of dreams in narrative, whereby a cluster of them in a work is deliberately interrelated. Such a complexity distinguishes Virgil from his Greek master. While the visions in Homer are discrete and without cross-references, Virgil's form a rich tapestry of meanings. Consider the very first dream in the *Aeneid*. The disguised Venus describes to Aeneas Dido's monitory dream of her assassinated husband, Sichaeus. It motivated Dido's flight westward, and her consequent founding of Carthage reminds the Roman reader of the great struggle to ensue long after. In presenting the love between Dido and Sichaeus, the relation of the dream prepares us also for her dilemma in Book IV and for her flight in Hades from Aeneas into her husband's arms. Moreover, it establishes a parallel to Aeneas's own career, as he too was propelled out of Troy by a dream of a dead and bloody phantom (Hector) urging flight from the homeland. This second vision – modelled on Achilles's of Patroclus – is related in the next book, through a fine irony, by Aeneas to Dido. It fuses the fall of Troy with the found-

---

[51] *Aeneid* iv. 465-474. A similar symbolic natural dream in Valerius Flaccus's *Argonautica* occurs at the inception, instead of the conclusion, of a love affair (trans. J. H. Mozley [London, 1934], v. 330-343; cf. Apollonius of Rhodes, trans. R. C. Seaton [London, 1912], iii. 615-645). Yet a third such dream occurs at the center and turning point of the love affair in Gottfried von Strassbourg's *Tristan* (trans. A. T. Hatto [Baltimore, 1960], pp. 219-220).

ing of Rome, thereby setting up a historical parellel to the establishment of Carthage.[52]

In Book IV, Aeneas tries to explain to Dido his sudden departure by mentioning the iterated dream of the troubled mute
ghost of Anchises; the hero has been so absorbed in his love that
he has not fully understood, until the daylight appearance of
Mercury, that action is required. Again the wraith of a departed
person in a dream propels Aeneas to his destiny, this time out of
the fires of love instead of the flames of Troy.[53]

The most complex and carefully interrelated cluster of dreams,
however, is found in Dante's *Purgatorio*. At the dawn after the
first night spent in Purgatory, Dante dreams that an eagle snatches
him up like a Ganymede to the fiery sphere. There he becomes so
hot that he awakens startled and pale, like Achilles after having
been brought by his mother to Scyros. Virgil informs him that
they are now in Purgatory proper because Lucy carried him up
while he slept. This dream is recognizably "realistic", with its
sensation of movement and flux: the dreamer is honored, terrified,
reassured, scalded. Although the subject of the canto is the pilgrim's crucial change of heart, the change as yet has happened
to him, beyond his will and understanding – Lucy (Grace, Contemplation), not Virgil, *carried him* up. The dream's eagle is a
symbol of baptismal regeneration, of the unearned divine aid
needed for growth of the spirit. The action of the canto is the
pilgrim's mysterious translation to a new realm and into a wider
mode of awareness. Such a change is suggested, symbolically, by
the allusions to Ganymede and Achilles; literally, by the trans-
ports of the soul freed from the flesh and wandering in a dream.

The second dream comes at the close of the second night. In
it appears an ugly, maimed Siren. As Dante gazes at her, she
becomes beautiful, begins to sing, and boasts of her powers of
satisfying men. A holy woman appears, at whose behest Virgil
rips off the Siren's clothing, whereupon the stench from the latter's belly awakens the dreamer. Virgil later explains to the pil-

---

[52]   *Aeneid* i. 353-60; ii. 268-302. This analysis of the two dreams is in-
debted to Messer, p. 9, and Steiner, pp. 24, 28-30.
[53]   *Aeneid* iv. 351-537.

grim that he should spurn the earth and turn to God, since those who yielded to the Siren are expiating in the next three terraces. This means that avarice, gluttony, and lust are due to sloth, from the cornice of which they have just come, and to sensual pleasure – the wiles of the Siren. The Siren, moreover, lies about having successfully lured Ulysses, because lying is a part of the sins of the flesh. At first non-functioning and impotent, she is a monstrosity warmed into illusory life and attractiveness by the attention and love the dreamer gives her. The ugly becomes attractive by being familiar. *She* has not changed, but Dante's senses and fantasy have changed her. Beauty is created in the eye of the beholder.

The significance of the dream is that the pilgrim's senses and intellect, properly receptive to the goods of this life, may transform the transient into the obsessive by dwelling too long on these goods. The wrong kind of love can be caused by disproportionate love or by an error of the senses, by that incorrect vision which makes the unattractive attractive. His moral sophistication, however, reveals the inadequacy of these delights as soon as their attraction is felt. The holy lady represents something intuitive, some innate moral sense using reason (Virgil). Dante has come a long way from the first dream, as Virgil appears *within* this vision; that is, Virgil's wisdom is now assimilated in Dante's own spirit. The pilgrim feels physically freer as well. Indeed on this day he will advance from Virgil's light to Beatrice's.

In the third dream, Leah gathers flowers for a garland while Rachel observes herself in a mirror. The one is a type of the active life, the other of the contemplative. Both Old Testament persons foreshadow the roles of Matilda and Beatrice in the Earthly Paradise, and, like Virgil oblivious of the Christian paradoxes, stand for the limited ideal of enlightened paganhood, for pastoral pleasures and beauty. Earthbound like the pagan, they appear only in a dream; similarly, after the dream, Virgil takes his leave of Dante, having prepared him for the entrance to Eden on this morning.[54]

[54] *Purgatorio,* trans. Thomas Okey (London, 1901), IX, 19-67; XVIII,145-XIX, 64; XXVII, 91-114.

All three visions are dreams as we know them but also contain truths not arrived at by conscious reasoning. They are almost evenly spaced through the *Purgatorio* and occur in a natural slumber after a day's strenuous climb, near the dawn. At night, sleep, the image of death and the old Adam, paralyzes the will and prevents the further climb up Purgatory and the further growth in awareness. Accepting the physical weakness, the spirit is freed for another mode of travel, free from confinements of the flesh, of discursive reason, of the moral will; it becomes aware, through visions which are symbolic and prophetic, of the next stage in the pilgrim's education. The dreams occur near the dawn because of the belief, arising in late antiquity and often alluded to by Dante, that then the spirit is most free and the dream prophetic. When sent by the mysterious power of love and received in a state of grace, such dreams were considered a minor species of revelation. They are necessary only in our post-lapsarian state; after the submersion in Lethe, Dante experiences four waking visions, and Beatrice tells him that he is no longer like one dreaming.

The dreams come at moments of decisive advances: at Purgatory's gate, at the beginning of the terraces of fleshly sins, at the entrance to the Earthly Paradise. As a sequence, they reveal a progression. The first one is egocentric, Dante being at the center of the action. In the following dream, Dante's error in judgment is corrected by the Virgil who appears within the vision. In the third dream, Dante is a witness and auditor. The progression from the Siren to the Old Testament ladies, moreover, prepares him for the sight of Beatrice and then of the Virgin. The incipient eroticism has been sublimated into detached observation of beauty.

Genetically, the dreams progress as well. The first one is an enactment by the fantasy of the sense response to being carried by Lucy. The cause acting on the body sets off a dream in the mind which reflects the cause. Thus too the impact of the morning sun creates the strong sensation of heat that awakens the dreamer in accordance with the process of magnification in dreams. The second dream reflects the medieval concept of the excesses of the "imaginazione". The third dream, an untroubled depiction of order, is in accord with Aquinas's idea of the agent intellect, which, equivalent to reason, is the activity of the soul with the products of the senses and the imagination. The meaning of the dreams is seen, as in the *Vita Nuova,* by hindsight; Virgil is an example of the wise man whom the dream theorists would have interpret the dream. In the second dream Dante is wiser and needs Virgil less; in the third one, he no longer needs him at all.

In sum, Dante has accepted the traditional teaching that we cannot know God and things divine without the help of sensible images. The dream, in Dante's psychology, serves to adumbrate with such images the truth not perceived perfectly with pure reason. All three dreams are part of a divine influx which, working through the imaginative faculty, gives them a veracious content and value as divination. Perhaps no one else in literature has devoted so much care to delineating the dream experience with such precision and such richness of meanings. This is not surprising, for he made all knowledge his province, and dreams seemed a valid source of knowledge in his age.[55]

---

[55] The analysis of the three dreams in the foregoing paragraphs owes much to the following two works: Francis Fergusson, *Dante's Drama of the Mind* (Princeton, 1953), pp. 30-42, 97-109, 161; Bernard Stambler, *Dante's Other World* (New York, 1957), pp. 115, 125, 184-194, 233-234, 240-241, 276, 285, 348-49, 357.

III

DREAM VISIONS IN SEVENTEENTH-CENTURY
ENGLISH LITERATURE

Having examined in Chapter I the outstanding philosophies of the
dream and their survival into the seventeenth century, and in
Chapter II representative examples of the major traditional kinds
of dreams as developed and used in various literary genres, I
now turn to the literature of the seventeenth century in order
to see how it carried on and modified the conventions at its
disposal. In the next three chapters, I will discuss each type of
dream, in the order in which they were taken up in Chapter II:
heuristic dream vision; love-dream lyric; ominous mantic dream
in drama; and monitory supernatural dream in narrative. Then
in Chapter VI, the survey will conclude with a study of Milton,
in whose work many types of dreams and their corresponding
literary genres are utilized with tact and often brought to perfection.

A. PSYCHOLOGICAL, AUTOBIOGRAPHICAL, PHILOSOPHICAL

After flourishing in the Middle Ages, the extended narrative set
within the frame of a dream became a minor genre in the English
Renaissance. Except for three works in the seventeenth century
– by Drummond, Donne, and Bunyan – which were, significant-
ly enough, in prose, the genre no longer served as a vehicle for
memorable expression by major poets. Instead, deliberately ar-
chaizing lesser writers like Drummond (as poet), Cowley, and
Henry More were attracted to it.

In examining these works we first take note of a masque by

Ben Jonson, *The Vision of Delight* (1617), which, though not
strictly a dream vision, is an enacting of the progression from
lower to higher visionary experience. The work begins as Delight
urges play and frolic. Invoked by Night, Phant'sie with its figures,
shapes, and airy forms enters next and brings dreams, true or
vain. Phant'sie is the healthy imagination – a product of "bloud,
and naught of fleame" – unchecked by reason and best known
to us in dreams, during which it frees us from the preoccupations
of the day. Yet it ushers in only an inchoate procession of formed and formless things, represented here by the dance of the An-
ti-Masque of Phantoms and Monsters, and by nonsense verses:

> If a Dreame should come in now, to make you afeard,
> With a Windmill on his head, and bells at his beard;
> Would you streight weare your spectacles, here, at your toes,
> And your boots o'your browes, and your spurs o'your nose?

Delight has been content so far to amuse itself with the pageant
of fantasy, with endless change and variety. This naturalistic
conception of joy yields to a fuller vision, as Houre, keeper of
Heaven's gate, leads in the Spring.[1] Such a change signifies the
mutability through which the world order fulfills itself. Thus the
masque utilizes "Phant'sie" and dream as metaphors for childish
delight in mere change, in escape from the everyday logic of
things. Something more than playful pleasure is, however, depict-
ed as central to life. Salubrious though insufficient, delight must
be complemented or transcended by a deeper emotion, wonder,
which looks beyond the ephemeral to the great natural changes
that are part of the eternal order. The masque thus dramatizes
the movement from mere dream vision to visionary insight.

A dream-vision poem proper is Cowley's short autobiographi-
cal "Complaint" (162 lines). The use of this form for an *apologia*
is, although not widespread, of long standing; there are interesting examples by Herodes, Ovid, Lucian.[2] Cowley's poem is con-

---

[1] Ben Jonson, *Works,* ed. C. H. Herford and P. Simpson (Oxford, 1925-
1947), VII, 461-473.
[2] See Herodes, *Mimes,* trans. J. M. Edmonds and A. D. Knox (London,
1929), p. 163; Ovid, *Tristia,* trans. A. L. Wheeler (London, 1931), pp. 391-

cerned with justifying his choice not – like Herodes and Ovid – of style or subject matter but of career – like Lucian. The poet lies underneath a yew "in a deep Vision's intellectual scene" when a muse appears "who oft in Lands of Vision plays". Beautiful as when she "in such a well-clothed Dream" appeared to "Pinder her Theban Favourite", she is glad to see that Cowley has returned to her at long last after years as a prodigal lost in political intrigue, business, and worldly affairs. His folly must be apparent to him now; the king has been restored and all should be well:

But whilst thy fellow Voyagers I see
All marcht up to possess the promised Land,
Thou still alone (alas) dost gaping stand,
Upon the naked Beach, upon the Barren Sand.

The poet replies by reviling the muse for having kidnapped him at birth. Making him sing when he should have ploughed, she hindered his worldly work. He can hardly overcome her influence: "Still thou dost Reign,/Lo, still in verse against thee I complain." He has finally come to see that to be happy one must reject her altogether; his great error has been to make himself a "demy-votary". The muse, moreover, should be the last to criticize the princes' slow rewards: "Thou . . . rewardest but with popular breath,/And that too after death".[3]

One of his best known poems, this is a charming personal allegory with overtures to an uninterested, ingrate Charles II. It combines the contents of the medieval poet's lament on his financial state – such as Chaucer's "Complaint to his Purse" – with the frame of the medieval dream vision. The latter form permits a personified muse to expound her ideas; she represents the artistic impulse within Cowley, which he half seriously, half tenderly scolds. He makes incidentally some perceptive comments on the irresistibility of the poetic impulse; on the difficulty of

---

397; Lucian, "The Dream, or Lucian's Career", in *Works,* trans. A. M. Harmon and K. Kilburn (London, 1913-1961), III, 219-33.

[3] Abraham Cowley, *Works,* ed. A. R. Waller (Cambridge, 1905-1906), II, 435-440.

heeding that impulse while also trying to make a living; on the rewards gleaned, through change of politics, by opportunists rather than men of integrity. Suffused with irony, the poem indicts not poetry but the society which scorns the spirit; the carefully placed reference to Pindar evokes the honor accorded the bard and his art by ancient society. This dream vision is thus not a minor document on the subject of the supposed "Restoration" of traditional values.[4]

Cowley uses the vision form also in a different sort of poem, "A Dreame of Elysium" (91 lines). As he falls asleep, the muse enters again, this time leading him on a visit to the Mansions of Felicity. He observes there renowned poets, heroes, and lovers kissing and dancing amidst perpetual joys, wines, flowers, songs. The traditional *locus amoenus* here celebrated is set in a dream because it is unavailable to the waking man. The work concludes by pointing the moral of the life-is-a-dream metaphor: when a cock crows, everything vanishes – so transient indeed are all earthly delights. Reaching for the disappearing muse, the poet grasps only air and shadows. He awakens grief-stricken, desirous of following her and of leaving the waking life in order to dream forever. "Thus chiefest Joyes glide with the swiftest streame,/And all our greatest pleasure's but a Dreame."[5]

A longer dream vision with a glimpse of another sort of ideal existence is William Drummond's "Song i" (252 lines). As the poem opens, the poet wanders with delight through the traditional medieval spring bloom. Amidst these pleasures, he halts and falls into a sleep in which a "Heaven of Visions in my Temples rolled". He beholds three naked nymphs who emerge from the myrtle and run to the brook. Of one, prettier than the rest, he takes special note. In his innocence he had not known of this weakness, love: "What wondrous thing is this that Beautie's named/(Said I) I finde I heretofore have dreamed?" Like the lover in Donne's "Good Morrow", he regards past joys, when

---

[4] John Hoskyns likewise uses the allegorical dream for an *apologia*, when committed to the Tower for making a speech against the king (*Life, Letters, and Writings*, ed. L. B. Osborn [New Haven, 1937], p. 206).

[5] Cowley, II, 42-44.

compared to his present bliss, as an unreal dream. Drummond's poem, however, contains the added irony that the present joy takes place in a dream; thus the present dream renders unreal the pleasures of the actual past.

The vision suddenly shifts, as the dreamer finds himself before a tower on a rock. It is the "Fort of Chastitie", closed to all who have left it once or who have seen their own faces in Venus's mirror. The poet-lover remains by a cypress shade outside, lamenting his unattainable Hope inside. As he glances in a brook, beholding there the changes wrought in his face by love, he awakens in fear. This change is no deliverance, "for what into my troubled Braine was painted,/I waking found that Time, and Place presented."[6]

In this poem, the unrequited lover's dream delineates the archetypal experience of falling in love with feminine beauty and the paradox of being attracted to and repulsed by chaste love. The dream frame seems natural in so medieval and allegorical a work. Nevertheless the poem's sudden shift breaks it in half, and the relation between the halves is not developed. The lushness of the language of description, moreover, has here become an end in itself; it wearies, whereas the descriptions of Drummond's master, Spenser, are confined to the significant moral details. Indeed to F. R. Fogle, the poem represents Drummond's most complete intoxication with sensuous physical beauty; without moral reflection, even with implied regret for the lady's chastity, it stands out as a specimen of late medieval and Renaissance celebration of earthly love.[7]

Drummond's "Song ii" (248 lines) is set in autumn and is at the other end of the love experience in scope, morality, and situation. The Petrarchan lady has died. In deep mourning, the poet does not fall asleep until the dawn sets "open wide the christal port of Dreames". A beautiful virgin seems to stand by his bed, urging him to cease mourning. Having recited a long list of reasons for

---

[6] William Drummond, *Poetical Works*, ed. L. E. Kastner (Manchester, 1913), I, 9-16.
[7] See F. R. Fogle, *A Critical Study of William Dummond* (New York, 1952), pp. 151-52.

rejoicing, she orders him to look up: "I live, and happier live, but thou art dead." The lover becomes aware that this is indeed his departed lady's spirit. The poem now changes from the delineation of personal grief into a detached survey of the human condition. Fame, love, wonder lead but to dust; the dreamer is urged to look to the immutable "world of perfect blisse". As he tries three times to reply to that familiar face, she vanishes "in Titan's light".[8]

So concludes a work which is a mixture of genres. The central situation is that of the Petrarchan sonnets and *canzoni,* wherein the lady reappears after death to comfort the lover. The form, however, turns into an extended impersonal meditation on the traditional *contemptus mundi* theme. "Song ii" marks the lady's last appearance to him and points to the splendors of the invisible world and heavenly love, even as "Song i" celebrates her first appearance in a context of earthly love and beauty. The dream frame is thus a common denominator of the two poems. "With some awareness, surely, of symmetry and pattern, he uses the same device" to depict the beginning and end of profane love.[9]

In its fusion of thought and feeling, its resolution of conflict into a clear vision, its solemn tone marking the transition from the poetry of love to the poetry of religious meditation, "Song ii" is one of Drummond's best poems. It is also an early version of his more extensive exercise in this genre, *A Cypress Grove,* one the great English prose works of the century.

The *Cypress Grove* discards entirely the personal love situation. It begins instead with observations on the soul's powers of divination. The poet retires for the evening but finds himself with troubled emotions for which, unlike the ones in "Song ii", there is no apparent cause. He supposes them ominous emblems of hidden destiny springing from the presaging power of the mind. Attempting to think of all probable sources of evil, he is brought

---

[8] Drummond, I, 65-72. For similar poems see John Norris, "The Grant" in *A Collection of Miscellanies* (London, 1706), pp. 94-95, and Patrick Hannay, "Sheretine and Mariana" included in *Minor Poets of the Caroline Period,* ed. George Saintsbury (Oxford, 1905-1921), I, 645-47.

[9] This paragraph is based in part on Fogle, pp. 155-57.

at last to the inevitable climax – the possibility of death. After this introduction, the work proper begins with reflections similar to those in "Song ii". A long sympathetic survey of the conventional arguments against the love of life and the fear of death is ended by the coming of dawn. Pacified, the persona falls asleep.

Just as Socrates in the *Republic*, upon concluding a complex line of reasoning, utilizes the vision of Er as a concrete image capable of arousing our emotions, so Drummond turns from waking speculations to a visionary sleep – "if sleep it may bee called, where the Mind awaking is carried with free wings from out fleshlie bondage". He seems now to be in a place from which he can behold everything: the moon, the earth, the great celestial spheres. A majestic man appears and orders him not to recall the earth with its opinions and fears, its dream-like existence. Contrasting its pettiness with the joys of heaven and the beatific vision, he explains the resurrection of the body, warns of Judgment and Eternity. "Which when Hee said (mee thought) He vanished, and I all astonished did awake".[10]

The form of *A Cypress Grove,* then, is partly of Platonic origin. The meditation is generated by troubling dreams and climaxed with a dream vision of ultimate reality. The latter is clearly modelled on the famous eschatological dreams deriving from Plato's Vision of Er: Scipio's in Cicero, Godfrey's in Tasso, and, indirectly, the *Commedia*. The work follows, furthermore, a certain sequence: it moves from an examination of the vanity of the human condition to a glimpse of the transcendent reality. This literary form, developed in the traditional medieval meditation, is common also to Donne's two "Anniversary" poems and *Devotions Upon Emergent Occasions,* and the fifth chapter of Browne's *Hydriotaphia*. In Drummond's version of the genre, there is a transition from Stoic consolation to the raptures of Christian Platonism. The dream at the end, arising naturally from the thoughts on mortality "limned" in his waking mind, is a type of revelation. It verifies and carries to a conclusion what

[10] Drummond, II, 67-100. For other eschatological dreams, see Chamberlayne's *Pharonnida* in Saintsbury, I, 64-69.

Drummond's thoughts – unaided nature – had established. The dream is Faith added to Reason, the numinous fulfilling the natural.

B. POLITICAL, POLEMICAL, SATIRICAL

The vision work was sometimes taken out of the realm of pure literature and used as invective or polemic in contemporary political quarrels. Thus Charles I's jester, Archy Armstrong, was responsible for a squib directed at Bishop Laud. Attached to the Royal Court, Archy showed his animus against Laud by jokingly suggesting, among other things, that the Archbishop often feasted on a dish of scholars' ears. When he composed the mock prayer, "Great praise be to God and little laud to the Devil", the Archbishop had him thrown out of court. Years later, with Laud in the Tower, Archy saw his chance and published, "A Choice Anthology of the Archbishop's Enormities entitled *Archy's Dreams*".[11] This trivial work represents one insignificant man's gloating.

An intellectually more imposing and consistently angry work is Cowley's "A Discourse by way of Vision, Concerning the government of Oliver Cromwell". We have already seen the discomfort Cowley came to feel about the Restoration; he had no doubts, however, of the malevolence of the Roundhead hegemony. In spite of admiration for Cromwell's courage, he hated the man; in fact, the "natural" basis for the poet's dream is his reluctant attendance at the funeral of the Protector. Rendered melancholy by the ceremonies, Cowley goes to sleep and falls "at last into this Vision, or if you please to call it but a Dream, I shall not take it ill, because the Father of Poets tells us, even Dreams too are from God".

He is transported to Mona top, where he bewails the past twenty years' martyrs. Suddenly a naked giant appears on whom

[11] *Archy's Dreams* (London, 1641) in *Ashbee's Facsimile Reprints* (London, n.d.). For similar political visions – Edward Pettit's *Vision of Purgatory* and *Visions of Government* – see G. F. Sensabaugh, *That Grand Whig Milton* (Stanford, 1952), pp. 118-19, 124.

are painted recent battles; he bears a bloody sword and, on his head, three crowns. The poet confronts the giant, who describes himself as a Principality (an order of angels) in charge of the British Isles. When a lengthy dispute breaks out between them, the dreamer becomes suspicious of the other's identity. The giant eulogizes Cromwell's undertakings as grand in scope and notably successful. The poet, alarmed at the Machiavellian language, realizes now whom he is facing; he remains calm, however, and pretends that the giant has merely been ironical. Reviewing the same list of achievements with sarcasm, he finds them but the wicked acts of a tyrant. When the giant menacingly approaches him, an angel bearing British crown and cross appears in a flash of light, pronounces an exorcism, and routs the monster.[12]

The dream frame allows, as in medieval allegory, for a debate by personified sets of ideas – in this case, Christian Humanism and the new secularist political viewpoint. The frame, however, contributes little to the force of the work. The ending is insipid and without reference to the dream; through most of the work, indeed, the reader is hardly aware of the dream. What makes the dialogue nevertheless bristle with excitement is the intellectual vigor of the debate. Basic political theories are brought into open conflict. The two sides are well characterized. If the giant reminds us physically of the Satan of *Paradise Lost,* intellectually he is cousin to the Satan of *Paradise Regained,* who likewise speaks the language of expediency, ignoring moral and religious reality. Analogous also is the giant in the frontispiece of Hobbes's *Leviathan,* who bears crown, sword, and crozier; both Cowley's and Hobbes's giants aspire to be the guardian "angels" of the state.

Success makes right – such a generalization may be a distortion of Machiavelli and Hobbes, but there are always those who, lacking the subtlety of these two thinkers, reduce political theory to the cliché. Cowley was thus giving voice to and exposing the secular spirit abroad in Europe, even as the Cambridge Platonists opposed it in a philosophical context. Brooding over the drift to

[12]   Cowley, II, 342-376.

anarchy after Cromwell's death, the poet assumed the role of a Hebrew prophet by writing a book of visions and denunciations. He thus adopted – or perhaps burlesqued – the visions of the very sectarians he was attacking. Cowley's sense of the interplay of ideas and of their distortion by shifts in word meanings and philosophic premises; his strong ironies and brisk colloquial style; his deft use of dramatic irony by beginning with a naive *persona* in whom there grows a deep awareness of the reality facing him – all contribute to make this, along with Dryden's *Essay of Dramatic Poesy,* one of the liveliest dialogues of ideas in the century.

While Cowley confined himself to political matters, Donne undertook in *Ignatius His Conclave* a broad critique of contemporary culture. At first, Donne probably wrote the satire in response to a purely political crisis in France only. But some time in 1610, Kepler's *Somnium* came into his hands. The problems presented by that work, as well as by the contemporary *Sidereus Nuncius* of Galileo, may have prompted the poet to enlarge the scope of his critique. The allusions to the latest innovators, Galileo and Kepler, occur only at the beginning and end of the work. It would therefore appear that on seeing the manuscript of Kepler's *Somnium,* he attached the frame of the dream trance and cosmic voyage to the earlier version, which had apparently been a series of dialogues in Hell (in the manner of Lucian) and aimed only at the Jesuits. As it now stands, *Ignatius* is a satire directly of the Jesuits and indirectly of the innovations wrought in medicine, cosmology, and political theory by the Renaissance. Although Donne appears to have had some sympathy for the pioneers of new ideas, he regarded their discoveries as disruptive.[13]

---

[13] The vexing question of the strata of composition in *Ignatius* is discussed in detail by Marjorie Hope Nicolson (*Science and Imagination* [Ithaca, 1956], pp. 67, 69-74) and C. M. Coffin (*John Donne and the New Philosophy* [New York, 1958], pp. 200-201, 204-210).

In its final form, *Ignatius* begins with a dream:

I was in an *Extasie,* and
> My little wandring sportful soule,
> Ghest, and companion of my body
had liberty to wander through all places, and to survey and reckon all
the roomes, and all the volumes of the heavens, and to comprehend
the situation, the dimensions . . . of the planets.

Leaving such scientific matter to the conceited innovators, Galileo, Kepler, and Brahe, the poet comes instead to Hell where
disembodied souls fly about. He observes Copernicus, Paracelsus,
and Machiavelli forwarding claims to the lieutenancy under Lucifer on the grounds of having introduced innovations into the
modern world. While Ignatius refutes their arguments by proving
that none of them has caused so much trouble as the Jesuits,
Lucifer attempts mediation by suggesting that the moon be
brought closer to the earth in order to transfer the Jesuits to it.
The Evil One hopes for an eventual union of the "Lunatique
Church" with the Roman and of Hell-on-Moon (as it would be
once the Jesuits populated it) with the older Hell. Just then a
fight erupts and the poet returns to his body, which is by now
refreshed.[14]

The cosmic voyage through the new Copernican universe –
the first such trip in English literature – is thus combined with
the very ancient motif of the journey to Hell. The satire of the
old Jesuits is fused with the satire of the new scientists; the
idea of sending the Jesuits to the newly proximate moon seems
a graphic way of wishing a plague on both their houses. Furthermore, Hell is here a type of Rome; Ignatius' attempt to oust
Boniface III adumbrates what might yet happen in Rome. The
work is thus a lively, vigorous, and imaginative satire of much
of contemporary culture and politics.

The dream trance knits the varied material together. Whether
Donne himself conceived of the dream or borrowed it from Kepler's *Somnium* is not important. More pertinent is the question

---

[14] Donne, *Complete Poetry and Selected Prose,* ed. J. Hayward (London,
1929), pp. 357-407.

of the kind he utilized, for his dream accords with the Stoic and Neoplatonic notion that in sleep the soul undertakes farflung voyages to obtain knowledge – in this case, the old secrets of Hell and a view of the new cosmology. Unlike most visions, such as Kepler's *Somnium,* in which the dreamer is usually passively observing the dream-action brought to him, this work delineates a true "ecstasy" – a journey outside the body. In fact, during Ignatius' long oration against Machiavelli, the poet fears that his body, so long abandoned by his soul, will putrify and be buried. When he awakes, however, his body feels refreshed because the Neoplatonic dream voyage has been successfully concluded "with new acquist of true experience".

C. MORAL AND RELIGIOUS

Kepler's *Somnium* influenced other works in seventeenth-century English literature besides Donne's *Ignatius.* One of these, Henry More's "Insomnium Philosophicum" (174 lines), introduces us to the moral and religious dream vision. Instead of satirizing the passing scene, this species deals with the eternal obstacles and rewards in the course of the Christian soldier's wayfaring.

More's poem begins, like Donne's work, with the active soul's separation from the body, in the manner of the Neoplatonic dream:

My weary body lay out-stretched, not I.
For I, alas! from that dead corse had fled. . . .
Free as in open Heaven, more swift than thought
In endless spaces up and down I flie.

This dream is a special vision in which the soul moves voluntarily, not flying on wings as men often do in "deceiving sleep/Hovering over Waters, Woods, and Valleys steep,/But born on the actual efflux of my will". More beholds an orb similar to the earth; one half contains fair inhabitants dwelling in the light of a sun, the other half bears foul people in the dark. The former, fully contented, smile and praise God's works; the latter rail with complaints and blasphemies. The poet soon awakes, aware that

it was a dream
But yet from dreams wise men sound truth may gather. . . .
But where, or heavy passions closed the eye,
Or prejudice, there's nothing can make wise.[15]

This allegorical vision is a curious blend of More's scientific imagination and his didactic earnestness. It uses the astronomical diagram to contrast beliefs about God held by the saved and the unregenerate. God's grace is represented in the Neoplatonic manner by the sun – called "Logos" – illuminating the universe; the shadow of night typifies the darkness of error. The idea of two kinds of creatures on an orb similar to our world is probably a borrowing from Kepler's *volvans* and *privolvans*. More's creatures, however, are given moral attributes: the objects of his attack, Puritan pessimists, wilfully turn away from God's benevolence and regard the world as evil. Thus through fantasy mankind sees itself as it might appear to an observer on another planet. From the dream we attain a detached view of our physical and spiritual world.[16]

While More uses astronomical knowledge for moral allegory, Bunyan appropriates for the same end the story of a journey. *Pilgrim's Progress* begins baldly with hardly any details of setting:

As I walked through the wilderness of this world, I lighted on a certain place where was a Den, and I laid me down in that place to sleep; and, as I slept, I dreamed a dream.

This abstract opening, of a man lying down anywhere, is rich in overtones. The phrase "the wilderness of this world" comes to us like an echo of the *Commedia*. The work is apparently going to be about the visionary experience of a sinner lost in the midst of this life. Secondly, the person wandering through the world and lying down to sleep in the wilderness is reminis-

[15] Henry More, *Philosophical Poems,* ed. G. Bullough (Manchester, 1931), pp. 144-49.
[16] This analysis of the poem is based on Nicolson, p. 77, and Bullough's notes in his edition of More, pp. 235-36.

cent of Piers Plowman and other seers of medieval vision. "Dreamed a dream", furthermore, has the proper Biblical resonance, maintained through the whole work.[17]

The story begins as though it were about a narrator who is the center of the allegory. Nevertheless a curious transfer takes place: "I dreamed, and behold, I saw a man ... with ... a great burden upon his back". The adventure begun by the narrator is started again in the same way *within* the dream, by the new person: "Now, I saw, upon a time, when he was walking." The narrator has suddenly dropped out of prominence in the story; but, although he becomes mainly passive, he never fully disappears. The work is filled with certain formulae which recur at regular intervals as if to remind us of the dream frame running parallel to the story: "I looked there and saw", "I saw moreover in my dream", etc. The last sentence of the book brings the narrator out of the dream and concludes the rectangular frame which contains the story: "So I awoke, and behold it was a dream." [18]

The narrator does not, however, remain entirely passive. Once in a while he moves on the periphery of the action for reasons not too clear. Thus when Help pulls Christian out of the Slough of Despond, the narrator enters his own dream in person – "Then I stepped to him that plucked him out" – and inquires why the road is kept in so bad a condition. On receiving an answer, the narrator disappears just as mysteriously. One wonders why Christian could not have been made to ask this question.

The most puzzling event occurs later in the story. Having taken Christian and his companion up the hill Clear to glance at Celestial City, several shepherds hand them a note and warn them to beware of sleeping on Enchanted Ground. "So I awoke from my dream",

---

[17]   John Bunyan, *The Pilgrim's Progress* (Oxford, 1902), p. 9. The situation in the Old English poem, "A Dream of the Rood", is also similar: the Christian dreams of the resplendent cross imparting to him the essentials of the faith and urging him to spread word of what he sees in the vision (included in *Anglo Saxon Poetry,* trans. R. K. Gordon [London, 1926], pp. 261-65).

[18]   Bunyan, pp. 9-13, 31, 52, 61, 62, 106, 159. Geoffrey Tillotson discusses briefly the rectangular frame of this work in "Dreams in English Literature", *Mercury* (1928), p. 520.

says the narrator at that point, "And I slept, and dreamed again." Although such an awakening and prompt resumption of the dream takes place often in *Piers Plowman,* this is the only occurrence of it in *Pilgrim's Progress.* It is the more vexing because it does not mark any change in the character of the pilgrimage. J. B. Wharey has suggested that the break is meant to mark Bunyan's release from prison.[19] Yet surely Bunyan would have been an incompetent writer to insert such a personal and extraneous allusion in so obscure a manner. Perhaps the answer lies elsewhere.

A theme of this work is sleep, physical (literal) and moral (figurative). Early in the story, Christian comes upon three men fast asleep: Simple, Sloth, Presumption. He awakens them and tries to remove their shackles, since they are in danger from the roaring lions. Replying blandly, however, to the perplexed Christian that there is no danger, they return to sleep. When in Part II, Christiana and Mercy pass by the same place, the three have been hanged by their iron fetters because they not only were themselves subject to sloth and folly but they also persuaded others to their way of life.[20]

After crossing the Hill Difficulty and studying the roll that is his promise of salvation, Christian himself falls asleep. The roll drops from him. Upon awakening, he pursues his way unaware of the accident. Only when facing new adversities and reaching for the roll does he discover his loss. He prays to God and chides himself for his folly in sleeping – especially in daytime and in the midst of difficulty. Again, when Christiana and Mercy pass by the same arbor, they rest but are careful not to fall into a like sinful sleep. Their guide explains that the forgetfulness of pilgrims causes some people to sleep when they should remain awake.[21]

After the adventure in Vanity Fair, Christian and Hopeful fall asleep on the grounds of the Giant Despair. He thereupon throws them into his dungeon. On escaping from that incarceration

[19] Bunyan, pp. 15, 120-21; J. B. Wharey makes the point in the notes to his edition of *Pilgrim's Progress* (Oxford, 1956), pp. 313, 333.
[20] Bunyan, pp. 38, 210-211.
[21] *Ibid.,* pp. 42-45, 57, 69, 213-14.

brought about by sleep and on arriving at the hill Clear, they are warned not to sleep on the Enchanted Ground still to be passed through. When they later reach that land, they indeed become drowsy; Hopeful even attempts to rationalize the taking of a short nap. They manage to remain awake only by singing:

When saints do sleepy grow, let them come hither . . .
Thus to keep ope their drowsy slumb'ring eyes.
Saints' fellowship, if it be managed well,
Keeps them awake, and that in spite of Hell.

Others are less successful; when Christiana and Mercy pass through the same grounds, they find Heedless and Too-bold fast asleep as a result of having seated themselves to rest for a while. The two women kindly attempt to awaken the men, who only stir and speak in their slumber. "This is the mischief of it", the guide comments, "when heedless ones go on pilgrimage. . . . This Enchanted Ground is one of the last refuges that the enemy to pilgrims has." It is the most difficult to come through because the weariness is greatest when the journey is nearly over. The two sleeping ones will lie here until they rot.[22]

In this work, then, sleep – which was to Prudentius and others a figure for the unregenerate life – functions as a metaphor for backsliding. The Christian journey is in some ways like a trip through the land of the lotos-eaters. The many external dangers, such as of beasts and giants, are not so difficult to overcome as the dangers from within, from the weakness of the spirit. Hence the fall of the people in the Enchanted Ground is central to the story:

Those that die here die of no violent distemper. The death which such die is not grievous to them; for he that goeth away in a sleep, be-gins that journey with desire and pleasure; yea, such acquiesce in the will of that disease.

Sleep is thus a form of moral and spiritual suicide. When Mercy's doubts of "missing" are finally removed, she is so joyous that

[22] Ibid., pp. 120, 133-34, 294, 296-99.

she cannot sleep. This is not only a "realistic" psychological detail: in Beulah (Heaven) there is no slumber at all. The pilgrims there cannot sleep because of the bells and trumpets, "yet they receive as much refreshing as if they had slept their sleep ever so soundly".[23]

For this reason, when he hears the stern command given Christian not to sleep on the Enchanted Ground – one of the climaxes of this theme – the dreamer-narrator is jolted awake. He is, after all, himself asleep. In other words, despite his passivity, he plays a role in the scheme of the allegory. He is unregenerate man looking on nonchalantly at the career of a soul in the process of regeneration. Since he has not full understanding of all that goes on, he rarely comments on what he sees. But the warning against sleep comes home to the detached slumbering spectator and pushes him into the moral drama.

Hence when Christian enters Beulah, the narrator makes one of his few entries into the story. "I looked in after them." He, the sleeper no longer passive, describes the golden city as though he were following Christian and then peeping in past the gates that close behind the hero. "I wished myself among them" – yes, he wishes this, but he has yet to undergo Christian's experience, and he perhaps does not comprehend all that that entails, in spite of his having beheld it. Hence, too, he awakes with an ignorance of the vision's meaning – which is irony on Bunyan's part, but not on the narrator's:

Now, reader, I have told my dream to thee;
See if thou canst interpret it to me.

It is equally significant that the last action of the story does not at all involve the Christian whom we have followed through the book. After the gates to Beulah close, we lose track of the hero

---

[23] Cf. Herrick's poem, "The White Island, or Place of the Blest", which describes the flight from this world – the Isle of Dreams – to eternity, where there are no monstrous fancies to fight and where the eyes are never steeped in sleep but attend to pleasures without end (*Works,* ed. L. C. Martin [Oxford, 1956], p. 376).

and observe instead the narrator who has been almost invisible throughout. "Now while I was gazing upon all these things, I turned my head...". He has, as it were, leaped into the story at the moment of seeing the City of Gold – the goal of the journey, and the only part of the story that the unregenerate can fully understand. He wants to enter it, unaware that the whole of Christian's ordeal has to be experienced at first hand. Just then he beholds "Ignorance come up to the river side"; not possessing a certificate, the new arrival is seized and dispatched to Hell. The story concludes at this point, that is, as the unregenerate narrator – the sleeper in this world – faces alternative conclusions. Whether he, and the reader, will turn out to be Ignorance or Christian remains uncertain.

We now see why the narrator awoke on that one occasion two thirds of the way through the tale. The warning against sleep had touched a tender nerve; the dream had become momentarily too relevant and frightening. Yet, as people often do when awakened by discomforting dreams, he turned over and resumed sleep and dream, jolted but still unregenerate. The narrator's role is thus a part of the story. He represents all sinners; he is the reader, everyman. His sleep, spanning the whole story, is so long that it may deceive us into ignoring its existence, yet the average life is likewise led in a "sleep" of which one is unaware by dint of its length and unbrokenness.

The narrator's slumber differs from ours, however, in one respect: it contains a special dream. The unregenerate narrator is given his private revelation in which the course to be followed is carefully charted out. This too is explicable in terms of the story's symbolic language. Not all sleep is entirely bad; in the Interpreter's house, for instance, Christian beholds a revealing incident: a frightened, trembling man rises out of bed and tells of a dream he has had of Judgment Day. The dream ended just as God peered at the dreamer, whose sins suddenly came to mind, whose conscience accused him, whose final judgment appeared near, but whose soul was not ready. The man, in receipt of his Revelation, changes his life accordingly. His dream affects Christian as well, who informs Piety that he is glad to have heard of it even though it makes his heart ache.[24] In Part II, Christiana is brought to her senses by a dream of like import.[25] In the same way, *Pilgrim's Progress* is the dream-revelation experienced by the reader and is meant to initiate the regenerative process in *his* life. Hence in the introductory verses, Bunyan says of this book to the reader: "Wouldst thou be in a dream, and yet not sleep?" The narrator's special dream, which corresponds to the dream of the man in Interpreter's house, becomes a waking revelation to us, the readers, whose option it now is to follow in the steps of Christian or to remain, like Ignorance and the many others, a passive "sleeper" of this world.

The dream-vision was not, then, entirely obsolete in the seventeenth century, even though it had ceased to be a major form of literary expression. Drummond's poems are perhaps too backward looking for our taste, too dependent on Petrarch, Tasso, Spenser. But in the visions of Donne and More we find new knowledge being assimilated into old forms; in Cowley's "Complaint" and "Vision ... Concerning ... Cromwell", as well as Donne's *Ignatius,* are vigorous critiques of the religious, political, and intellectual transformations of the seventeenth century; and Bunyan's *Pilgrim's Progress* is an artfully constructed, carefully integrated parable of which the dream is not only the frame but also part of the content and theme.

---

[24] Bunyan, pp. 35-36, 47. Christiana is likewise shown the man at the Interpreter's house and told of his dream (p. 196).
[25] The same happens to Mercy later on. Indeed the dream is close to Bunyan's terrifying nightmares, related in *Grace Abounding,* ed. G. B. Harrison (London, 1928), pp. 5, 20-21.

IV

DREAMS IN SEVENTEENTH-CENTURY ENGLISH LYRIC POETRY

Dreams are occasionally described and commented on in seventeenth-century lyric poems. The dream's function here is not, as in vision works, to convey esoteric lore or frame a narrative but to dramatize a relationship, express a state of mind, depict a person or place. By far the greater part of such poetry is given over to love dreams, in which the poet celebrates his lady's attractiveness, delineates his hopeless passion, or sketches the consummation so devoutly wished. But there are as well other kinds of dream poems, and I will begin with an examination of lyrics based on, or referring to, Neoplatonic and Stoic ideas of dream journeys and *sympatheia*. Turning then to the widespread love dream, I will examine its use in complimentary or genteel love poems; in ratiocinative and satiric verses; and, finally, in deliberately voluptuous lyrics.

A. "NEOPLATONIC" AND "STOIC"

Although virtually every writer of amatory poetry essayed the love dream, several lyrists interested in the dream phenomenon itself referred to dream experiences in other than love poetry. I indicated in Chapter I how men like Sir Thomas Browne, Owen Felltham, and Thomas Tryon articulated some of the old Neoplatonic and Stoic ideas of dream-journeys and heuristic dreams; several poets of the late sixteenth and seventeenth centuries, influenced by Renaissance Neoplatonism, likewise took inspiration from these beliefs. George Chapman, for instance, speaks at times of the soul's wanderings in sleep. Anticipating in his "Hymnus in Noctem" – a poem celebrating the powers of night – the arrival of darkness and dreams, the poet asks to have his senses bound by slumber so that the soul, "wanting but franchisement and memory/To reach all secrets", may be loosed. Night brings gifts: "From the silk vapours of her ivory port,/Sweet Protean dreams she sends of every sort:/Some taking forms of princes", others of dead friends or beautiful ladies who revive us:

But from the Night's port of Horn she greets our eyes
With graver dreams inspired with prophecies,
Which oft presage to us succeeding chances,
We proving that awake, they show in trances.[1]

Later Neoplatonic poets like Lord Herbert of Cherbury, Vaughan, and Traherne wrote in quite similar terms of the soul's activity in dreams.[2] Concurrently, among sixteenth and seventeenth-century poets not directly influenced by Neoplatonism, the theory of the soul's traveling during sleep became the justification of lyrics which tried to diminish the pains of parting. Such poems asserted or implied that while the bodies separate, the souls, in some sort of *sympatheia,* communicate most readily through dreams.

This genre was commonplace among the Elizabethans; Shakespeare, for instance, wrote several such sonnets among those pertaining to his absence from his Friend. In one, the poet accuses the Friend of breaking his sleep,

While shadows like to thee do mock my sight.
Is it thy spirit thou send'st from thee
So far from home into my deeds to pry?

The poet recognizes, nevertheless, that it is "mine own true love that does my rest defeat" (1xi). Another poem is built on the paradox that he sees best when he "winks"; the Friend appears

---

[1] George Chapman, *Poems,* ed. Phyllis Bartlet (London, 1941), pp. 25, 27.
[2] Lord Herbert of Cherbury, "To His Mistress", in *Poems,* ed. G. C. Moore Smith (Oxford, 1923), p. 49; Henry Vaughan, *Works,* ed. L. C. Martin (Oxford, Second Ed., 1957), pp. 48, 74, 286, 292, 304-305; Thomas Traherne, "Dreams", in *Centuries, Poems, and Thanksgivings,* ed. H. M. Margoliouth (Oxford, 1958), I, 138-139.

most clearly in dreams. "All days are nights to see till I see thee,/And nights, bright days when dream do show thee" (xliii). The pain of awakening from such a dream is suggested by a metaphor in the couplet of another sonnet: "Thus have I had thee, as a dream doth flatter,/In sleep a king, but waking no such matter" (lxxxvii).[3]

So Donne too wrote in Elegy XII, "His Parting from Her":

Rend us in sunder, thou canst not divide
Our bodies so, but that our souls are ty'd,
And we can love by letters still and gifts,
And thoughts and dreams; Love never wanteth shifts.

A moving passage in Elegy XVI, "On His Mistress", supposedly dramatizing an actual separation, tries to comfort the poet's distraught wife by asking her to dream well of him – "augur me better chance". If she vexes herself over his absence, she will be haunted by nightmares, which might bring actual harm to him. "When I am gone, dreame me some happiness" rather than

　　　　　in bed fright thy Nurse
With midnight startings, crying out, oh, oh,
Nurse, oh my love is slaine, I saw him goe
O'er the white Alpes alone; I saw him I,
Assail'd, fight, taken, stabb'd, bleed, fall, and die.[4]

Later in the seventeenth century, William Browne articulated the same notion in an epistle to a friend: he spends his day with various cares, and at night

　　　　　by the kindness of a happy dream,
Enjoy what most I wish; yourself and such. . . .
In sleep I walk with you, and do obtain
A seeming conference: but, alas, what pain

---

[3]   William Shakespeare, *Works*, ed. Hardin Craig (New York, 1951), pp. 481, 478, 486.

[4]   John Donne, *Poems*, ed. H. J. C. Grierson (Oxford, 1912), I, 103, 112. For similar lyrics written earlier in the sixteenth century, see Surrey's poems xvii and xix in *Silver Poets of the Sixteenth Century*, ed. G. Bullett (London, 1947), pp. 124, 127.

Endures that man, which evermore is taking
His joys in sleep, and is most wretched waking? [5]

Cowley's "Friendship in Absense" is more detailed and better poetry:

When chance or cruel business parts us two,
     What do our souls I wonder do?
     Whilst sleep does our dull Bodies tie
     Methinks, at home they should not stay,
     Content with Dreams, but boldly flie
Abroad, and meet each other half the way.

Sure they do meet, enjoy each other there,
     And mix I know not How, nor Where.
     Their friendly Lights together twine,
     Though we perceive't not to be so,
     Like loving stars which oft combine,
Yet not themselves their own conjunctions know.[6]

That is, the soul of the true friend, instead of remaining content with passive dreams, undertakes the active dream-journeys delineated by the Neoplatonists and Stoics.

It is but a slight extension of this theme to suggest that souls can overcome the greatest of separations – death – which is, as often iterated, closely related to sleep. Thus in his epicede *Elisa,* Phineas Fletcher depicts a woman meeting her late husband in a dream. Thinking he yet lives and embraces her, she eagerly queries him about his absence:

  Strong delight her dream and joy defaced;
But then she willing sleeps; sleep glad receives her;
And she as glad of sleep, that with such shapes deceives her.[7]

[5] William Browne, "An Epistle" in *Poems,* ed. G. Goodwin (London, 1894), II, 236.
[6] Abraham Cowley, *Works,* ed. A. R. Waller (Cambridge, 1905-1906), I, 27.
[7] Giles and Phineas Fletcher, *Poetical Works,* ed. F. S. Boas (Cambridge, 1908-1909), II, 283. Other verses describing dream appearances of the dead are by William Chamberlayne ("Pharonnida", in *Minor Poets of the Caroline Period,* ed. G. Saintsbury [Oxford, 1905-1921], I, 172); Thomas Flatman ("Urania", III, 364); Katherine Philips ("Songs from *Pompey"*, I, 611).

B. THE LOVE-DREAM LYRIC (I): COMPLIMENTARY AND GENTEEL

Such random use of dreams in the lyric were dwarfed, however, by the prevalence of love-dream poems. The genre, growing out of Petrarch and the Renaissance tradition, had been very popular in sixteenth-century European poetry. In the *topos* common to these poems, the lover usually dreams that his cruel lady has relented and come to solace him, but sleep forsakes him just as he is about to enjoy this godsend. As Mario Praz points out, this basic situation is often adorned with a complaint addressed to sleep, a description of the lady, the presence of a mythological figure, or with quibbles on the rise of the "other" sun in the dead of night.[8] Once fully awakened, the poet wishes himself able to sleep thus forever; so Lovelace puts it:

Thus poets who all Night in blest Heavens dwell,
Are called next morn to their true living Hell,
And what substantial Riches I possess,
I must to these unvalued Dreams confesse.[9]

The lament at having to arise from such bliss is often sounded. Wither experienced a dream so full of joy that

   to possess what to embrace I seem'd
Could not affect my joy in higher measure
Than now it grieves me that I have but dreamed.
Oh, let my dreams be sighs and tears hereafter,
So I that sleeping weep, may wake in laughter. . . .
Might all my dreams be such, oh, let me never
Awake again, but sleep and dream for ever.

Since the aftermath of joyful dreams is a sense of unendurable hopelessness, he would make his eyes "forswear for ever sleeping" were he to know that the "next night had such dreams in keeping".[10]

---

[8] Mario Praz, "Donne and the Poetry of his Time", in *A Garland for John Donne,* ed. T. Spencer (Cambridge, Mass., 1930), p. 53.
[9] Richard Lovelace, "The Triumphs" in *Poems,* ed. C. H. Wilkinson (Oxford, 1930), p. 174.
[10] George Wither, "Fair Virtue" in *Poems,* ed. F. Sidgwick (London, 1902), II, 61.

But not all love dreams were delightful. Thomas Stanley spoke of one which, because dreams are the image of life, set his jealous soul at strife:

I saw, when last I closed my eyes,
Celinda stoop t'another's will;
If specious Apprehension kill
What would the truth without disguise?
The joys which I should call mine own,
Methought this rival did possess.

All his happiness is like a dream, yet dreams themselves allow him no happiness. In another poem, Philip Ayres sees his beloved appear in mourning dress. As they hold each other tearfully, she responds to his questions only with sighs:

[I] grasped her fast, she struggling to be gone,
Till wak'd [sic]: but then I found myself alone.

Oft have I grieved to think what this might prove,
And gathered hence ill omens to my Love;
But since I may too soon the mischief find,
I'll strive to chase the fancy from my mind.[11]

If the lover suffers from displeasing dreams, he is sometimes unchivalrous enough to wish the like on his lady. William Drummond, for instance, asks the moon ("who paints strange Figures in the slumbring Braine") to show the lady "these Tears, and the black Mappe of all my woe". Since the lady will not heed the lover, perhaps a dream of him will bring him to her attention.[12]

In a similar vein, Edmund Waller apostrophizes a dream he has had of his Sacharissa. The dream image is friendly enough to him; for that reason, however, the unrequited lover is in anguish: "But ah! this image is too kind/To be other than a dream." The real Sacharissa, it seems, was never so kind. He therefore

---

[11]   Thomas Stanley, "The Dream", in Saintsbury, III, 133; Philip Ayres. "A Dream", II, 294.
[12]   William Drummond, "Sonnet x" in *Poetical Works,* ed. L. B. Kastner (Manchester, 1913), I, 8. Other poems in which dreams are wished on the beloved are Katherine Philips' "Songs from *Pompey"*, in Saintsbury, I, 611; William Browne, *Works,* II, 29-32, 201.

requests the vision to represent a pale, wan, despised lover, "then to that matchless nymph appear/ ... Softly in her sleeping ear,/ With humble words, express my woe." Surprised, she will perhaps desist from her pride. The poem has enacted a neat turn-about from the dream he has had to the dream he wishes her to experience.[13]

The genteel love-dream lyric tended to shade off imperceptibly into the quasi-religious. John Norris's "Sleep" begins in the conventional manner, by urging Morpheus to bring repose to the lover's weeping eyes and melancholy heart:

But do not all my senses bind,
Nor fetter up too close my mind;
Let mimic Fancy wake, and freely rove,
And bring th'Idea of the Saint I love. ....
Summon the best Ideas t'appear
And bring that Form which most resembles her.

If none is as fair as she, let Morpheus's painter, Fancy, "limn/ The form anew and send it by a dream"; he can repair to the lover's heart, "for sure her Image is not worn out there". While this poem retains the language and setting of the conventional love-dream lyric, such words as "Idea", "Form", "Image", "Saint" give it a Platonic or religious flavor not inapposite to it were it addressed to the Virgin.[14]

Among seventeenth-century poets, Herrick wrote the largest number of dream lyrics. Not all such poems are directly related to the love dream: we note the Heraclitean observation in the two-line poem "Dreams":

Here we are all, by day; by night w'are hurl'd
By dreames, each one, into a several world.[15]

Another classical theme appears in "A Country Life", which depicts in a Horatian and Martialesque manner the pleasures

---

[13]   Edmund Waller, "Say, Lovely Dream!" in *Poems,* ed. G. Thorn Drury (London, 1904), I, 53-54.
[14]   John Norris, *A Collection of Miscellanies* (London, 1706), pp. 92-93.
[15]   Robert Herrick, *Works,* ed. L. C. Martin (Oxford, 1956), p. 21; for Heraclitus see p. 500.

of retired country life. Such a clean waking existence at the
side of a chaste wife is marked "with those deeds done by day,
which ne'er affright/Thy silken slumbers in the night." The pleasant dreams, of natural scenes and Elysian calm, are yet not so
ecstatic as to enamor the dreamer of sleep and detain him from
his daily tasks.[16]

In his miniaturist's way, Herrick uses the old idea of the
transmigration of poetic power. In "Visions" he dreams he sees
Anacreon – with flushed face and vine-leaves in his hair – lisp-
ing, reeling, tippling. Finding him too drunk to make love to her,
an enchantress removes his crown in anger and gives it to the
dreamer, who has since become dizzy, wild, wanton, and – though
he does not say so explicitly in the poem – a poet of pleasure.
Herrick here uses the dream to account for the major influence
on his poetry, even as Ennius declared himself a disciple of Homer by similar means.[17]

Another group of dreams is about Love (Eros, Cupid), who
appears to the poet as part of a miniature allegory in the manner
of Hellenistic lyrics.[18] Among Herrick's more erotic dreams is the
"Vision of Elektra", in which he dreams of being on a bed of
roses with his lady. Rejecting his amorous advances because,
as she says, the faults of the night would blush by day, she
allows him only to kiss her. He is not granted even that much
in the "Vision", wherein a huntress with Spartan dress and thighs
bared like Diana's rebukes the dreamer as too coarse for love.[19]

---

[16] *Ibid.*, p. 36. For other remarks on dreams in a rustic setting, see John
Chalkhill's "Thealma" and Patrick Carey's "The Country Life", in Saintsbury, II, 376, 465.

[17] Herrick, pp. 313, 563. For Ennius see *Remains of Old Latin*, trans. E.
H. Warmington (London, 1935), I, 3-9.

[18] See Chapter II, section C, for a brief survey of these ancient love-
dream lyrics. For other seventeenth-century uses of Cupid, see Shakerly
Marmion's *Legend of Cupid*, in which the little god displaces Satan as a
malevolent cause of dreams (in Saintsbury, II, 12); Kynaston, on the other
hand, substitutes fairies for the Devil or Cupid ("Leonline and Sydanis",
p. 137).

[19] Herrick, pp. 20, 51; other Herrick love-dream lyrics are on pp. 16,
219, 279. For poems similar to these see Drummond's Sonnet xlvii and
Madrigal ix (*Works*, I, 42, 46), and Sidney Godolphin's "Fair Shadow,
Stay", (in Saintsbury, II, 240).

In most of these dream lyrics, the lover is that unique combination of naivety, desire, diffidence, and charm characteristic of the *personae* of Herrick's other amatory poetry.

C. THE LOVE-DREAM LYRIC (II): RATIOCINATIVE AND SATIRIC

The best love poet of the century, Donne, did not use the love dream extensively, but it appears in a characteristically concentrated and super-subtle form in two poems. Both are called "The Dream", one included in the *Songs and Sonets,* the other among the Elegies. The interpretation of Elegy X has been complicated by the fact that the title, added later, is probably incorrect. Grierson points out that it should be called "The Picture", because the first eight lines – which assert that the image of his beloved is so impressed on his heart as to make him her medal – are about a picture of the lady rather than about a dream. In line 9, the discussion shifts to the dream state. The lover tells the lady that when she departs along with Reason – the waking state – Fantasy (dreams) presents "meaner" and more "convenient" joys. By locking up sense, shutting out pain and truth, Sleep brings consummation of his passion. Epistemologically, there is no distinction between waking and dreamed-of pleasure; if he but dreams he has her, he indeed has her, since "all our joys are but fantastical".

In line twenty-one, however, he abruptly changes his mind by asking her to stay. Even though during her physical presence "our joys at best are dreame enough" and though she leaves him all too soon, he prefers waking pain in the presence of his haughty beloved to the illusory joy of dreams. Notwithstanding that both experiences are equally transitory, he would rather be "mad with much heart" – maddened by emotional pain during the actual presence of the unrequiting Lady – than be "ideot with none", bereft of "Reason" in slumber. The dream experience is an advantage to him that the lover willingly rejects.[20]

[20]   Donne, I, 95; see II, 77, for Grierson's analysis of the poem.

Donne's reasoning typically twists and turns itself as he examines his emotions from every point of view. This contorted logic is even more characteristic of the lyric included in the *Songs and Sonets*. The poet awakens from a love dream of his lady and beholds her before him:

Dear love, for nothing less than thee
Would I have broke this happy dream,
    It was a theme
For reason, much too strong for fantasy,
Therefore thou waked'st me wisely; yet
My dream thou brok'st not, but continued'st it.

Maria Praz has pointed to Donne's typical resuscitation of a weary convention through departure from it; the alteration is apparent in the very first lines: the poet on awakening no longer addresses a rhetorical complaint to an obscure beauty vaguely identified with the rising sun but speaks directly to his beloved actually present in the room. The poem contains therefore a dramatic quality absent from the lyric effusions of the usual love-dream verses; each stanza, moreover, is a little scene with a changing action of its own.[21]

The lover is glad to be awakened out of a happy dream because its burden – the love play – is more suitable for waking action ("a theme for reason") than for a sleeper's fantasy. The sophistical, logic-chopping style of compliment and suasion then begins, followed by the sensual lover's practical conclusion to this scholastic reasoning: "Let's act the rest." The drama takes a new turn in the third stanza as she rises, apparently unconvinced by his dialectic. The skillful lover turns even this setback into matter for logical triumph. Her rising now to leave makes him doubt that it was she at all; he then gives a self-deceptive rationalization of her action, as though to talk her and himself into believing that the situation is not so bad as her leaving would suggest:

Perchance as torches which must ready be,

[21] *Ibid.,* I, 37-38; this analysis is based on that of Mario Praz in Spencer, pp. 55-56.

Men light and put out, so thou deal'st with me,
Thou cam'st to kindle, goest to come.

The poem concludes as the lover speaks of dreaming – literally
or figuratively – of "that hope" again. Unlike the usual love-
dream poem, its end, like its beginning, seems optimistic, but his
rationalizing and hair-splitting have won him the argument rather
than his mistress.

In this lyric, the dream ecstasy is in the background. Alluded
to at the beginning, it occurred in the past and may recur later.
The body of the poem is concerned with the brief events that take
place in the wake of the dream: the lady's short visit and abrupt
departure after rejecting his advances. Yet on this simple event
Donne has built a superstructure of paradoxes, sophistry, and
blandishments. He has introduced the question of the relationship
of dreams and waking reality to happiness, and the possibility of
reaching an accord of all three.

Most important of all, while the usual love-dream poem merely
contrasts the sleeping bliss with the sad actuality, Donne has put
the dream to work as a means of fulfilling itself in reality. He
uses it as an additional and potent weapon in the siege of his
beloved. Consequently, even though there are some similarities
of idea and expression with Elegy X, the lyric differs substan-
tively from that work. This lover, neither woebegone nor resigned
to waking pain, not so sure that waking "joys are but fantastical"
nor willing to choose between waking pain and unreal joy, prefers
rather to realize the dream. In the lover's eagerness to improve
his lot by action, this poem not only differs from the more usual
love-dream lyrics but is also an outstanding example of Donne's
own kind of unsentimental, "tough-minded" love verses. Indeed
the failure of the lover's ingenious attempt nearly turns the poem
into a satire aimed at the lover himself.

When the love-dream poem had become widespread in the
English Renaissance and the genre had undergone such complicated refinements, it was only natural that the rising tide of satire
in the latter two-thirds of the century should sling a few shafts in
its direction as well. In their idiosyncratic, highly wrought style,

Donne's two poems contain the seeds of self-parody. His strained attempt to express complex feelings did not have to be pushed far before its ingenuity became ridiculous, its far-fetched similes and fallacious logic became a word game. Thus John Cleveland was as much influenced by Donne as was Herbert or Marvell. In his "To the State of Love, or the Senses' Festival", Cleveland turned upon the love-dream convention. "I saw a vision yesterday", the poem begins conventionally enough, but the next line alters the tone: "Enough to sate a Seeker's sight". In the midst of a love-dream lyric appears the language of social satire. "It was a She so glittering bright/You'd think her soul an Adamite." After a description full of such far-fetched similes, the poem concludes – when the cockcrowing effaces the dream just as the lovers' bodies are joined – on the punning question, "Who would not die upon the spot?"[22]

While Cleveland dissolved the conventional situation in gales of words and conceits, Samuel Butler, truer to the vein of mock heroic, retained the passionate language but rendered the situation trivial by reducing it to a love affair between cats. In the middle of the night, Puss dreams of trysts and gallantry amid fagot-piles or in garrets:

And, as in Dreams Love's Raptures are more taking,
Than all their actual Enjoyments waking,
His amourous Passion grew to that Extream,
His Dream itself awak'd him from his Dream.
Thought he, what Place is this! or whither art
Thou vanished from me, Mistress of my Heart?
But now, I had her in this very Place,
Here, fast imprison'd in my glad Embrace,
And, while my Joys beyond themselves were rapt,
I know not how, nor whither thou'rt escap'd.[23]

If we were not told that these lines pertain to cats, we would think them from a conventional love poem. What is curious about this poem and its author is that Butler, an early charac-

---

[22]   In Saintsbury, III, 19-21.
[23]   Samuel Butler, "Repartees between Cat and Puss ..." in *Satires,* ed. R. Lamar (Cambridge, 1928), p. 135.

teristic figure of the Enlightenment, was notoriously skeptical of enthusiasm in religion, politics, and love. Every alleged passion was to him a delusion or malevolent hypocrisy. Writing here well within the love-dream convention, however, he allows his feelings esthetic outlet for perhaps the only time – but in burlesque setting in the manner of Chaucer. One suspects that he indulged such sentimentality only when the context would reassure the reader, as well as himself, that this was merely meant to be ridiculous and could not possibly be mistaken for tenderness on his part.

D. THE LOVE-DREAM LYRIC (III): VOLUPTUOUS

We have so far examined the love-dream lyric as used for compliment; for genteel, so-called Platonic or Petrarchan love-making; for ratiocinative examination of one's emotions; and for satire of language or situation. There remains the love-dream lyric which celebrates the consummation of the amatory passion. Although the above genres might hint at that goal, they disguise or displace it with other interests relating to the battle of the sexes. But in the voluptuous dream lyric, the lover's intentions are clear. The poet's response may range from articulation of the experienced bliss – whether or not the dream reflects, or has a chance of corresponding to, reality – to *double entendre* and outright pornographic description.

These frankly voluptuous lyrics are of course common in the Restoration period. Even a stolid personality like Dryden, whose best verse is free of the erotic, bowed to contemporary taste when writing for the stage. In the midst of the heroic ardors of the *Conquest of Granada,* for instance, he inserted a lyric of questionable moral import, "The Zambra Dance". As the lover sleeps under a myrtle, Phyllis appears to him undressed. She meets his amorous advances with the assertion that she would rather "die" than lose virginity's "name". Her pun and her qualification intimate her real intentions; she speaks faintly and with a smile, as though without conviction. He soon has his way with her.

I waked, and straight I knew
I loved so well, it made my dream prove true:
Fancy, the kinder Mistress of the two,
Fancy had done what Phyllis would not do!

His conclusion is different from Donne's attempt to make the
dream a reality or (in Elegy X) to prefer the painful reality to
the dreaming joy: Dryden's lover warns Phyllis that despite her
haughtiness he can have his joy of her at least in dreams, no
matter what she does.

Ah, Cruel Nymph! cease your disdain;
While I can dream, you scorn in vain:
Asleep or waking, you must ease my pain.[24]

He accepts the dream joy as substitute for real consummation
– a compromise Donne's lovers, in the two love-dream poems,
would not make.

Dryden's fellow worker in the newly rising genre of neo-
classical satire, John Oldham, tried his hand at some erotic
poems of varying intensity. In "The Dream", the lover beholds
the *topos* common to such poetry – a shady grove by a stream
under a spreading tree. He sits there with his dear Cosmelia, his
hands roving through the "labyrinths of love". Urging her to
surrender, he begins to name "the thing . . . but stopt and blushed
methought in the Dream". He advances while she struggles faintly;
she at first checks his boldness but soon yields by pressing his
hand. "Hand pulled to, what t'other did remove:/So feeble are the
strugglings, and so weak/In sleep we seem." She asks him to
"forbear" even as she embraces him tightly: "Ah! do not, do not,
do not – let me go." Oldham articulates the climax with a mis-
chievous simile of the visions of holy men and with a secular
use of "ecstasy":

What followed was above the power of Verse,
Above the reach of Fancy to rehearse:
Not dying Saints enjoy such Extasies,

[24] John Dryden, *Poetical Works,* ed. G. R. Noyes (Second Ed., Cambridge, Mass., 1950), p. 63.

When they in Vision antedate their Bliss;
Not Dreams of a young prophet are so blest,
When holy Trances first inspire his Breast,
And God enters there to be a guest.[25]

Another Restoration wit, Rochester, reverses the sex of the
dreamer. A shepherdess lies asleep in a pigsty, where the grunt-
ing of the pigs inspires a dream. In it she sees herself busy with
pails as an unrequited swain-lover comes up begging her to help
rescue a pig lost in a cave. She rushes to the cave with him, but,
when they get there, he assaults her.[26]

The woman's dream is carried one step further by John Hoskyns. Addressing the "nimble dreams" (who "represent a world
of things/With much adoe and little paine") that visit ladies, he
delivers himself of a wish:

Howe highlie am I bound to you
(Safe Messengers of Secresie)
That made my Mrs. thynke on mee
Iust in the place where I would be.

O that you would [me] once preferr
To be in place of one of you
That I might goe to visitt her
And shee might sweare her dream was true.[27]

This is stronger stuff than the mild visions that the genteel love-
dream poets wish upon their ladies. Indirectly, it is a caustic
remark on the content of women's dreams; directly, it expresses
a hope to realize the dream by displacing it.

A consequence of love requited and fulfilled might be happy

---

[25]   John Oldham, *Works* (London, 6th ed., 1703), III, 374.
[26]   Some versions add a stanza which gives a naturalistic cause of the
dream:
   Frighted she wakes, and waking Friggs.
       Nature thus kindly eas'd,
   In Dreams rais'd by her murmuring Piggs,
   And her own Thumb between her Leggs,
       She innocent and pleas'd.
Rochester, *Works,* ed. J. Hayward (London, 1926), p. 24.
[27]   John Hoskyns, *Works,* ed. L. B. Osborn (New Haven, 1937), p. 189.

dreams experienced by the lovers in unison. Carew's "Rapture", an invitation to licentiousness, holds forth to the lady fine prospects for both the waking consciousness and the dreaming psyche. The poet invites her to Love's Elysium where, after active love play, they will lie down on a soft place "that so our slumbers, may in dreames have leisure,/To tell the nimble fancie our past pleasure" – the dreams will reflect their past activities and review the rush of delight too intense to be absorbed by the waking consciousness.[28]

An unusual erotic poem by Herrick brings ingenuity and quasi-Freudian fantasy to the usual literal seduction scene common in the genre.

I dream'd this mortal part of mine
Was Metamorphozed to a Vine;
Which crawling one and every way,
Enthrall'd my dainty Lucia.

Her legs, belly, buttocks, waist, neck, and hands are embraced by it. She can no longer stir; all parts are "made one prisoner". In the manner of such dreams, however, the rude awakening comes as he reaches the climax:

But when I crept with leaves to hide
Those parts, which maids keep unespy'd,
Such fleeting pleasures there I took,
That with the fancie I awoke;
And found (Ah me!) this flesh of mine
More like a Stock, then like a Vine.[29]

This poem's charm lies in the candid, naive manner of articulation, for Herrick's lover somehow remains innocent and genteel even when dealing with scabrous matters. The dream itself

[28] Thomas Carew, *Poems,* ed. R. Dunlap (Oxford, 1949), p. 50. Cf. Tom Brown: "Thus our happy lovers, after they have paid repeated obligations to love, lie intranced in one another's arms, and act over in their busy dreams the delicious scene that so transported 'em waking" (*Amusements,* ed. A. L. Hayward [London, 1927], p. 132). For love-dream lyrics by Carew's friend, John Suckling, see *Works,* ed. A. H. Thompson (London, 1910), pp. 18, 51-52, 61-62.
[29] Herrick, pp. 16-17.

has a certain "realistic" quality; it is a fine evocation of a sub-conscious male (or a child's conscious) erotic fantasy of extending physical delight beyond all limits. The wish fulfillment, shaped by the inner censor, takes a surrealist course that seems more credibly dream-like than any literal representation could be.

Last to be examined is a poem written early in the century by Ben Jonson that is one of the most satisfying of such dream lyrics even though its content is elusive. Some poems emphasize the power of the dream experience without giving any substantive details; of such a kind is Thomas Stanley's:

That I might ever dream thus! that some power
To my eternal sleep would join this hour!
So, willingly deceived, I might possess
In seeming joys a real happiness.
Haste not away: oh do not dissipate
A pleasure thou so lately didst create!

Although the bliss of the dream is conveyed, we have no way of knowing that it has anything to do with love. The last two lines not only inform us of that, but also bring a neat twist to the end – a demand on reality somewhat similar to Hoskyns's:

Stay, welcome Sleep; be even here confined;
Or if thou wilt away, leave her behind.[30]

Jonson's poem is a minor masterpiece of such indirection. Undone in the night by Love – with whom he has had nothing to do here-tofore – the poet does not know the object of this new emotion. He is left to find out in another slumber who the beauty is, but sleep does not return. What we have here is common in everyday life: a deeply satisfying dream, of which we recall in the morning only the joy, without the action or dream-content that gave rise to the emotion. It is an eery feeling.[31]

Based, then, on this common experience, Jonson's lyric adopts the old mythology of Love and personifies Sleep. There is no lady

[30]   In Saintsbury, III, 102.
[31]   Cf. Dante's use of this experience to convey the sense of the beat-ific vision at the climax of his work: *Paradiso*, XXXIII, 58-63.

in this dream because there is no remembered dream-content; the poet is only aware of a deep excitement which extinguishes further slumber. The desire to master the elusive sleep, as though that would continue the original dream, is particularly true to nature. In spite, or perhaps because, of its vagueness, this short poem is more suggestive and expressive of dream experience than many of the highly detailed love-dream lyrics. It not only is "one of Jonson's most happily inspired and most happily expressed fancies";[32] with Donne's lyric "Dream", Herrick's "Vine", and Milton's Sonnet 23, it is one of the best love-dream lyrics in the English Renaissance.

The Dreame

Or Scorne, or pittie on me take,
I must the true Relation make,
   I am undone to Night;
Love in a subtile Dreame disguized,
   Hath both my heart and me surprized,
Whom never yet he durst attempt awake;
Nor will he tell me for whose sake
      He did me the Delight,
        Or Spight,
   But leaves me to inquire,
   In all my wild desire,
      Of sleepe againe, who was his Aid;
      And sleepe so guiltie and afraid,
As since he dares not come within my sight.

---

[32] Ben Jonson, *Works,* ed. C. H. Herford and P. Simpson (Oxford, 1925-1947), VIII, 150; the quotation, by Swinburne, is in XI, 54.

V

DREAMS IN SEVENTEENTH-CENTURY ENGLISH DRAMATIC AND NARRATIVE WORKS

The dream in dramatic and narrative works functions as a means of motivating character, foreshadowing the inevitable, or creating suspense. It sometimes verges on the erotic, at other times approximates the heuristic dream of vision works. It is distinguished from these two genres, however, by its role as a brief interlude within a larger unfolding story and by its impact on plot and *personae*. It may counsel, guide, motivate, warn, prophesy, or demand revenge. Occasionally referred to later in the story, it may also be part of a carefully interrelated and contrasting series of visions. Finally, the dream's celestial or infernal provenience is sometimes indicated, as it rarely is in vision work or lyric.

I will survey first the use of dreams by Shakespeare, then by other dramatists of the seventeenth century. In the last section, I examine the dreams in several narratives and conclude with the Biblical epics which led to *Paradise Lost*.

A. SHAKESPEARE

The word "dream" occurs frequently in Shakespeare's works. He uses it in all its transferred meanings and in every kind of metaphorical expression to articulate diverse moods. He depicts also a rich variety of actual dreams. Often he treats them objectively, as avenues of occult information to the soul. Even the primitive type of objective divine-guidance dream is several times presented by him on the stage. This kind occurs, strangely enough, in the late plays, perhaps because of the increased interest in stage masques during the Jacobean years. Posthumus in *Cymbeline,* for example, experiences a dream of Jupiter informing him that all will be well. Diana appears to the hero of *Pericles* in similar fashion.[1]

There are many mantic dreams as well. Hector is urged on all sides not to fight the Greeks because of others' recent ominous visions. Brabantio dreams of something untoward just before he hears of Desdemona's elopement; when his daughter cannot be found, he abandons his doubt of Iago's story, and his dream is abruptly rendered mantic.[2] So Humphrey, Stanley, Romeo, Posthumus, Calpurnia, Cinna, Andromache dream more wisely than they know. Frequently "the testimony of dreams is ... authenticated by subsequent events",[3] as Shakespeare utilizes them (among other omens) to forebode and anticipate.

His use of old-fashioned objective and mantic visions leads him once to an exercise in archaeological reconstruction. In *Cymbeline* a Roman soothsayer is asked by soldiers what he has dreamed concerning the outcome of the impending war. The soothsayer, having fasted and prayed, is shown by the gods an eagle in a dream. He concludes that, unless his own sins have disturbed his powers of divination, this symbol of the empire bodes success for the Romans. The scene has a properly archaic tone. The interpretation, however, turns out to be false, like many another in Shakespeare. At the end of the play, the soothsayer does some verbal juggling to show that the dream's "real" import – the reconcilement of Caesar and Cymbeline – has come true.[4]

Such an event seems to present dream interpreters as fallible men. Other incidents in Shakespeare's works reinforce this impression. Having dreamed of a silver basin, a nobleman in *Timon*

---

[1]   William Shakespeare, *Works,* ed. Hardin Craig (New York, 1951), *Cymb.,* V, iv, 29-150; *Per.,* V, i, 240-250. For other objective dreams see *W.T.,* III, iii, 15-46; *H.VIII,* IV, ii, 80-94.

[2]   *Troi.,* V, iii, 6-10; *Oth.,* I, i, 143.

[3]   Sister Miriam J. Rauh, *Shakespeare's Use of the Arts of Language* (New York, 1947), pp. 94-95. Shakespeare's revitalizing of the dream tradition is remarked by Wolfgang Clemen, *Kommentar zu Shakespeares Richard III* (Göttingen, 1957), p. 160.

[4]   *Cymb.,* IV, ii, 345-353; V, v, 466-476.

of Athens anticipates another gift from the generous hero; but the latter's servant arrives to borrow, rather than to give, money.[5] Most interesting is the scene in *Julius Caesar* on the Ides of March. Caesar tells Decius that he is not going out that day because of Calpurnia's ominous dream. Shakespeare deviates at this point from his source, Plutarch. The Greek writer's Decius ridicules the dream and asks what Caesar's enemies would say if the Senate were to be adjourned to meet again when Calpurnia experienced better dreams. Shakespeare's Decius uses this argument also yet feels compelled to accept the seriousness of the dream, twisting it, however, in order to interpret it in a benign sense. Thus while Plutarch's Caesar is rendered vulnerable by his skepticism, Shakespeare's, on the contrary, falls by allowing himself to be beguiled with a sophisticated figurative interpretation – by contraries – which actually still implies Caesar's death. The symbolic dream here, as in *Cymbeline*, is truly mantic, but the interpretation is again misleading.[6]

Shakespeare's use of the love vision is not so frequent as one might expect. Several characters remark on the way amorous affection pursues its course by dreams and such unreal things. A few lovers speak of their total preoccupation, sleeping or waking, with the beloved. Charged with being "false in bed", Imogen adopts the language of the accusation and replies that her activity "in bed" consisted of thinking of her distant husband and, if asleep, breaking the slumber "with a fearful dream of him/ ... cry[ing] myself awake". The one fully described love dream in Shakespeare, however, actually never took place. Iago tells Othello that in sleep Cassio uttered loving expressions directed at Desdemona and kissed and handled Iago as though his bedmate were indeed the Moor's wife. This false story, ably contrived, makes an impact on the hero.[7]

---

[5] *Tim.,* III, i, 1-21. The dream is correct by contraries but is not correctly interpreted. For other examples of dubious dream interpretation see *Dream,* IV, i, 210-211; *2 H.IV,* II, ii, 92-99.

[6] *Caesar,* II, ii, 75-99; Plutarch, *Parallel Lives,* trans. "John Dryden" (New York, n.d.), *Caesar* 1xiii.

[7] *Cymb.,* III, iv, 45-46; *Oth.,* III, iii, 413-429. Lest we score Othello's credulity, we should remember that such things happened in literature, if

When Iago feigns a desire to soothe the aroused Othello by saying that it was only a dream in Cassio's mind, the Moor replies that it "denoted a foregone conclusion", that is, it reflected an already fulfilled desire and was not just "wish-fulfillment". This remark leads us to Shakespeare's interest in the psychology of the subjective dream. He depicts some dreams that contrast sharply with waking life. Certainly this is the burden of Caliban's story: strange sounds on the isle put him to sleep and,

> in dreaming,
> The clouds methought would open and show riches
> Ready to drop upon me, that, when I waked,
> I cried to dream again.[8]

Such dreams are the only escape from this dreamer's wretched existence – even as they are in the life of the unrequited lover (in the lyrics of Chapter IV).

Shakespeare presents as well other dreams that directly reflect the waking life. Tullus Aufidius, having always been defeated by Coriolanus, awakens exhausted from visions of wrestling vigorously with his arch-enemy. Hotspur is another soldier who dreams of war and battle to the point of perspiring in his sleep. The miserly Shylock dreams of money bags; the *persona* of the sonnets often has visions of his dear Friend while on a journey away from him.[9]

The relation of waking thoughts to dreams is most minutely described in Mercutio's famous speech. His examples – lovers dreaming of love, courtiers of courtesies and suits, lawyers of fees, ladies of kisses, parsons of plural benefices, soldiers of

---

not in life: cf., e.g., Longus, *Daphnis and Chloe,* trans. G. Thornley (London, 1916), iii. 9. For other references to the love dream see *Dream,* I, i, 154; *2H.VI,* I, i, 26; *Romeo,* V, i, 1-10. Love dreams are discussed by W. G. Meader, *Courtship in Shakespeare* (New York, 1954), pp. 13-4.
[8] *Temp.,* III, ii, 143-152; see also *Much,* II, i, 358-360, for another contrast between a dream and the character of the dreamer.
[9] *Cor.,* IV, v, 127-132, *1 H.IV,* II, iii, 50-65; *Merch.,* II, v, 18. See Chapter IV for sonnets 43, 61, 87, which describe dreams that directly reflect the events of the dreamer's waking life.

battles and drink – are the common ones cited by Lucretius, Petronius, Claudian, and Chaucer. New here is Shakespeare's use of Celtic folklore to give a whimsical cause to these dreams: Queen Mab's chariot generates them when touching delicate parts, such as ladies' lips or lawyers' fingers. By juxtaposing so fantastic a theory with a prosaic account of the way the subject matter of dreams reflects waking activities, Shakespeare has created the enchantment of these lines – lines which in themselves have little to do with the plot or the character who utters them.

When Romeo complains that Mercutio talks of nothing, the latter, having allegedly dreamed that "dreamers often lie", articulates the strongest skepticism found in Shakespeare on this subject:

> True, I talk of dreams,
> Which are the children of an idle brain,
> Begot of nothing but vain fantasy,
> Which is as thin of substance as the air.

But this remark, at the opposite pole from Shakespeare's objective and mantic dreams, does not necessarily represent the dramatist's beliefs: Romeo's ominous dream, mention of which aroused Mercutio's scorn, eventually comes true. He later dreams, moreover, that he is found dead by Juliet, revived by her kisses, and turned into an emperor; although regarding it a strange vision, he relishes it as showing that even love's shadows are possessed with joy. This dream too is fulfilled with tragic irony.[10]

Romeo's two ominous visions and Mercutio's *jeu d'esprit* make *Romeo and Juliet* one of the half-dozen Shakespearean plays in which dreams take a prominent part. Another of the six, *Julius Caesar*, contains, besides Calpurnia's dream and Cae-

---

[10]   *Romeo*, I, iv, 49-100; V, i, 1-10. Romeo believes that dreams hold "things true" and are "love's shadows"; his own dream turns out to be unfortunately all too true – by the principle of contraries. The dream reverses the position of the lovers in the Friar's subsequent plan. Even more ironical is the fact that it is partly realized when Juliet recovers and sees Romeo dead; but her kisses bring on a reunion in death, not his resuscitation.

sar's ambivalent response to it, Brutus's famous metaphor of the nightmare:

Between the acting of a dreadful thing
And the first motion, all the interim is
Like a phantasma, or a hideous dream.[11]

A third play, *2 Henry VI*, presents, in addition to several alleged (and perhaps feigned) mantic dreams, a striking scene between the capable but hated regent Gloucester and his ambitious wife Eleanor. He experiences an ominous symbolic vision, which he reveals only when she promises to relate her own morning dream. Each one then interprets both dreams in accord with his or her character traits.[12]

A Midsummer Night's Dream is the Shakespearean play richest in comic references to vagaries of the dream experience. The action takes place mainly at night; the characters frequently fall asleep. The very title, the opening lines, the subsequent references to dreams of love and to the brevity of all dreams are casual allusions introducing us to the important parts of the theme. Hermia experiences a semi-mantic dream in Act II. Thinking a snake crawls about her breast, she awakens to find herself abandoned by her fiancé Lysander. When the manipulations by Oberon and Puck begin, we are treated to many scenes of characters falling asleep and awakening with desires (or environment) altered. Eventually Puck brings the lovers back to normality by means of the magic juice, so that when they awaken, all the confusion seems but the fierce vexation of "a dream and fruitless vision". As the lovers are re-aligned, Demetrius, unsure whether they have been asleep or awake, proposes that during their return to Athens they recount their "dreams", that is, their previous loves and misadventures. Bottom then awakens out of *his* rare experience. He is certain that it was a dream beyond explanation,

[11] Brutus also urges Lucius to sleep, because the boy's slumber will be without the fantasies that busy care creates in men (II, i, 63-65, 231-32). Moreover, Cinna's ominous dream is quickly fulfilled (III, iii). *Caesar* is indeed one of Shakespeare's dream-haunted plays.
[12] *2 H.VI*, I, ii, 22-55.

which he intends to depict in a ballad to be called "Bottom's Dream". Thus the rustic domesticates and parodies what the well-born lovers had said of their own experiences.

In sum, the action of the play presents the unreal and flighty love passion in terms of the dream. Each change in the lover's affection reduces the reality of his previous devotion and precipitates an uncertainty as to his true amatory allegiance. Well might Puck say, "What fools these mortals be", after observing the dream-like inconsistency of the lover. In the epilogue, Puck turns to the audience and invites it to believe that it had slept and dreamed of the shadows of this play: the drama itself is like life, but a dream in which reality and fantasy are strangely mingled.[13]

The most dream-laden play in Shakespeare's canon is *Richard III*. At the very outset Richard informs us that he has spread rumors of mantic dreams incriminating his brother Clarence, who is indeed soon incarcerated because Edward IV "hearkens after" omens. So dream-haunted is this play that, although the dream that "G" will kill Edward's heirs is a feigned one, it nevertheless comes true – Gloucester, instead of George (Clarence), being the culprit. Here misplaced credulity leads to injustice; Hastings, on the other hand, when informed by Stanley of an ominous symbolic warning dream, ridicules any confidence in "the mockery of unquiet slumbers". The audience, readily recalling the suddenness with which Clarence's vision came true, sees the irony of the situation. Hastings soon thereafter changes his mind about such matters, but only as he is being led off to execution.[14]

In the meantime, old Queen Margaret's curse on Richard – that his sleep be broken with tormenting dreams and ugly devils – appears to be realizing itself. Richard's wife Anne mentions that she has not slept much since living with Richard, because

---

[13]   *Dream*, I, i, 8, 144, 154; II, ii, 147; III, ii, 371; IV, i, 72, 78-83, 198, 203, 208-221; V, i, 393, 430-435.

[14]   *R. III*, I, i, 33, 54; ii, 122; III, ii, 11-30; III, iv, 81-95. Clemen points out that Hastings' last words function as a commentary on the action; indeed, "tumble ... into ... the deep" recalls Clarence's dream (pp. 184-85, 196). Stanley, by the way, is one of the few Shakespearean characters to heed a dream – and thereby save himself.

his "timorous dreams" often awaken her.[15] We behold one example of them towards the end of the play.

Before turning to that, however, let us examine first the famous dream of the imprisoned Clarence in Act I. It falls into three sections. In the first, Clarence, apparently freed, is travelling at sea with his brother Richard and reminiscing over the War of the Roses. Suddenly Richard stumbles and, as Clarence tries to help him, his brother pushes him into the sea. What we have so far is a realistic natural reflection of Clarence's wish to be free, mingled with a fear of the consequences of involvement in the political scramble outside the Tower. But to the audience, informed of Richard's plan, this dream is a traditional mantic one.

The second section articulates the pains of drowning and, in iridescent verse, the response to exotic vistas at the bottom of the sea. The sight of wrecked ships, lost treasures, gems glowing inside skulls, human remains gnawed by fish provides a grim reminder of the medieval "ubi sunt" and "danse macabre" themes, as well as a judgment – like Godfrey's dream in Tasso – on the vanities that impel men. A realistic touch is Clarence's attempt to give up the ghost, which the sea holds in; he appears, in this agony, unable either to die or wake. Such a suffocating experience, part of the well-known incubus dream, is also an ironic foreshadowing of his death by drowning in the Malmsey butt.

The third part of the dream deals with the period after death. Passing the Styx into Hades, Clarence's soul enters a perpetual tempest. His previous victims, Warwick and the Prince of Wales, approach and accuse him of perjury and treachery. Some fiends then surround him; they howl so loudly that he awakens trembling. For a while he believes himself still in Hell, "such terrible impression made the dream".

Viewed as a whole, Clarence's dream covers past, present, and future, albeit in richly symbolic language. The first part presents his apprehensions about the future; the second comments

---

[15]   R. III, I, iii, 226; IV, i, 84-85. Richard himself later speaks of the two princes as his "sleep's disturbers" (IV, ii, 73).

on the vanity of the political scramble of the present, in which Clarence has participated and fallen victim; the third part looks to his past sins with remorse. At the same time, the dream moves from the concrete circumstances of Clarence's life to an unknown future; from a seacrossing to Burgundy, to another sort of water crossing towards Hell and Furies; from a wished-for freedom to an ironic freedom found in death.[16] The last part of the dream, furthermore, recapitulates dramatic material by recalling Clarence's guilt and the evils of internecine war.

There is much recapitulation in *Richard III* because of the complicated relationships working themselves out from the Henry VI plays. Shakespeare turned the dream into a means, among others, of such summarizing. This is even truer of Richard's unusual dream (in Act V), which begins objectively with a procession of his eleven victims. They appear and rail at him in the order of their deaths, reviewing crime by crime the whole tetralogy and concurrently comforting Richmond at the other end of the stage by praying for his success. Richard awakens with a start from a scene of battle, then realizes that he has only been dreaming. The blue light of the candles, however, certifies the presence of ghosts. He argues himself finally into indifference, conceding nevertheless that many voices in his conscience accuse him.[17]

The consequences of the two guilt-ridden dreams are interesting. Recalling the evil he has caused Margaret and her son, Clarence feels impelled to pray. This act, in addition to his repentant talk with the murderers, contrasts with that of the remorseless Richard, who awakens defiantly: bidden by the ghosts to despair and die, the king calls for a horse. Although admitting to fear of the voices within, he somehow anesthetizes himself so that by the time he rallies his men he can say, "Let not our babbling dreams affront our souls". He proceeds to condemn conscience, perhaps more to reassure himself than to edify his soldiers.

We have, then, besides the example of a feigned dream, a

---

[16]   This analysis of Clarence's dream (I, iv, 1-65) is based in part on Clemen, pp. 99-111.

[17]   *R. III,* V, iii, 118-206, 212-218, 227-233, 308.

four-fold view of dreams in this play: the happy dream of good Richmond, who arises refreshed and ready; the conscience-struck (and mantic) dream of Clarence, a sinner open to a regeneration made possible by the vision of his sinful past; Stanley's warning dream as applied to Hastings, a sinner "too fond" to heed a warning; and the dream of the utterly depraved Richard III on whom the judgment of God is clear.

Shakespeare's artistry is to the fore in these dreams: the grand stage spectacle of the ghosts; the manner in which the traditional objective dream is turned in the case of Richard into a realistic and prophetic subjective one; and, above all, the scope of Clarence's dream. Entirely of Shakespeare's invention, the latter is the longest and most beautiful in his poetic corpus. Although its middle section, the seascape, is not necessary for either mantic or recapitulative purposes, Shakespeare evokes – through concrete sensuous description – a vision of life under the aspect of eternity, a vision that transcends the immediate petty quarrels of politicians and sinful men.

Shakespeare used the recapitulation dream in other plays as well. A daring and exciting variation on it is Lady Macbeth's somnambulism. One of the high points of the Shakespearean use of dreams, it climaxes a play that, like *Richard III,* is full of prophecies, usurpation, murder, troubled sleep, and visions. While both Macbeth and Banquo dream "the cursed thoughts that nature/ Gives way to in repose", only Macbeth heeds their promptings. As he proceeds to the slaying of Duncan, the world seems to him wrapped in darkness, death, and "wicked dreams" which abuse sleep. He in turn is partly impeded in the killing when two men cry "Murder!" in their slumber. The tableau of this scene is thus of a dream-ridden Macbeth – who will be even more dream-haunted after his crime – proceeding, upon parting from a Banquo equally disturbed by visions, to a murder during which the nearby sleepers are assailed by evil dreams such as those Macbeth has himself mentioned moments before.

With Duncan out of the way, Macbeth's thoughts turn to Banquo, whose living presence causes the murderer to live in uncertainty and to be shaken nightly with "terrible dreams". After the slaying of his second victim, Macbeth's nightmares represent the gnawings of conscience rather than promptings to evil, as is indicated by his wife's subsequent reassurances to him, in the sleepwalking scene, that "Banquo's buried."

Macbeth has "murdered sleep", and now Lady Macbeth walks and talks in her sleep as if she were awake. With its completely confused time sequence, her subjective dream is a reflection of her twisted mind. Every allusion is to some incident in the past and thus testifies to the jarring impact her deeds have had on her consciousness. Her words, full of dark imagery, indicate fear and a desire to be rid of guilt but no actual remorse or repentance. Much richer than any mere dream of foreshadowing, her dream signals the completion of the reversal in the roles of Macbeth and his wife. She who had been of tougher fiber breaks down, while he becomes totally insensitive and unscrupulous.[18] If *A Midsummer Night's Dream* be a comic treatment of the life-is-a-dream outlook, *Macbeth* presents the converse of the same theme: life as a nightmare.

In *Antony and Cleopatra* another, less lugubrious, recapitulation dream becomes the subject of hyperbole on the relation between the ideal and reality. After Antony's death, his mistress tells of her dream of an Emperor Antony in all his glory; this is, we realize, mere wish-fulfillment and regret. After describing the dream person, she concludes that he was nature's masterpiece against fancy, that the reality of Antony transcended any idealization the dream could fashion.[19] This account of an alleged dream serves as a resumé of Antony's character and of Cleopatra's deep love for him – at last pure, without qualification or coyness. A means for hyperbole, as well as a useful alternative device to the soliloquy, the dream allows Cleopatra to articulate her inmost thoughts naturally. In beholding the break-up of her world, she confuses past reality with illusions and expresses her mood in terms of a dream. Without impact on plot or character,

---

[18]   *Macb.*, II, i, 8-9; III, ii, 17; V, i, 1-88. This analysis is based on Aerol Arnold, "Recapitulation Dream in *R. III* and *Macbeth*", *SQ* (1955), pp. 51-56.
[19]   *Antony*, V, ii, 74-99.

her remark functions perhaps more as a metaphor than as the narration of an actual dream.

Shakespeare makes many such brilliant metaphoric uses of the dream. For example, as Falstaff, expecting (in *2 Henry IV*) great boons, approaches the newly-crowned Henry V, the king turns upon him and says:

> I have long dreamed of such a kind of man,
> So surfeit swelled, so old and so profane;
> But, being awaked, I do despise my dream.[20]

This speech has the effect of distancing Henry's previous life. By redeeming time, the king turns his riotous past into an unreal episode and Falstaff's anticipations of the future into a mere dream.

Yet, beyond Brutus's nightmare of hesitations and Hamlet's "ambitions", beyond Falstaff's expectations and Hal's early prodigality, all of our natural life may be a dream; Shakespeare expresses on two different occasions the traditional life-as-a-dream metaphor in superb poetry:

> Thou hast nor youth nor age,
> But, as it were, an after dinner's sleep,
> Dreaming on both;

for

> we are such stuff
> As dreams are made on, and our little life
> Is rounded with a sleep.[21]

B. SEVENTEENTH-CENTURY DRAMA

Of dreams in other seventeenth-century drama not much need be said here because the subject has been covered in a monograph.[22] As in the literature from Chaucer to Shakespeare, God,

[20] *2 H. IV*, V, v, 53-55.
[21] *Meas.*, III, i, 32-34; *Temp.*, IV, i, 157-159.
[22] Jürgen Struve, *Das Traummotiv im Englischen Drama des XVII. Jahrhunderts* (Heidelberg, 1913).

angels, living human beings, ghosts of the dead, or beasts with human traits appeared in dreams. Although the causes of the dreams varied, the earlier playwrights of the century depended mainly on dreams generated by religious or mythological figures (e.g., Queen Mab), the later ones on natural dreams. Nightmares prophetic of evil were sometimes belittled and usually feared; but in the latter part of the century, dreams portending good fortune became common. The ancient belief that the mantic dream was experienced only by a prominent person obtained throughout sixteenth-century drama and fell into discard thereafter. On the other hand, the Germanic belief in women's, especially widows', susceptibility to dreams was still in evidence, as was the idea, current in late antiquity, that morning dreams were valid.[23]

An old genre appearing less frequently in the seventeenth century was that of the objective apparition of the vindictive dead: an example is in Marston's *Antonio's Revenge,* whose hero tells of two ghosts crying in his sleep for vengeance; when he tried to embrace them he awakened and noted great prodigies in the sky.[24] The mantic dream *per se* – without clear indication of its provenience – did not decline. A famous instance of it appears in Webster's *White Devil;*[25] likewise in Denham's *Sophy,* a princess describes an iterated dream in which she saw her husband near destruction. When, in spite of the prince's reassurances, she remains despondent, he says: "At night I shall resolve that doubt, and make/Thy dreams more pleasing." She experiences nevertheless more such nightmares:

[23] This paragraph is based on Struve's conclusions (pp. 35, 42-45, 81-84, 90-91, 95-99, 100-103).

[24] It should be noted, however, that a secondary character greets this awesome story by relating an even more portentous dream that – as the narration of it in prose indicates – is obviously a parody of the conventional serious dream (John Marston, *Plays,* ed. H. H. Wood [London, 1934], I, iii, 38-75).

[25] Vittoria, soon to give herself to the Duke by arrangement with her brother, seems in her own dream to sit under a yew tree. When she is confronted by her husband and the Duke's wife, a whirlwind arises and slays the latter two. Apprised of the dream, the Duke interprets it as a sign that Vittoria will prosper with him. It actually has no impact on the play's action but is a kind of dumbshow of what soon takes place (John Webster, *The White Devil,* ed. J. R. Brown [Cambridge, 1960], I, ii, 228-268).

But sure tis more than fancy.
Either our guardian Angels, or the gods
Inspire us, or some natural instinct
Fore-tells approaching dangers.

The dreams indeed prove true.

Another dream in the *Sophy* leads us to the category of natural dreams. When the Caliph claims that Mahomet revealed at night the prince's plans to slay the King, a defender of the prince slights the holy man's dream,

Because his crazy stomach wants concoction,
And breeds ill fumes; or his melancholy spleen
Sends up phantastick vapours to his brain:
Dreams are but dreams.

As letters implicating the prince are then intercepted, the king speaks with deliberate irony to the defender:

Alas, my fears are causeless, and ungrounded,
Fantastick dreams, and melancholick fumes
Of crazy stomachs, and distempered brains:
Has this convinced you?[26]

The prince is, however, innocent. Similarly a melancholy person in Otway's *Orphan* and the evil King Philip in his *Don Carlos* are subject to "animal" dreams which reveal the state of their minds.[27]

References to love dreams are often brief. A character in a Jonson play thinks that the tell-tale mark of a lover is his raving in sleep. Someone in the *Silent Woman* advises a suitor to "invent excellent dreams to flatter her". *Volpone* contains an amusing feigned dream in the scene in which the harassed Volpone tries to be rid of the loquacious Lady Politick Would Be; he alleges

[26]   John Denham, *Works,* ed. T. H. Banks (New Haven, 1928), I, ii, 113; III, i, 52-59, 131-137, 165-169.
[27]   Philip's sleep is constantly disturbed by dreams of the evil acts he has committed. When his accomplice, the Duchess of Eboli, enters, he guesses that her dreams have been as terrifying as his own. (Thomas Otway, *Plays,* ed. R. Noel [London, n.d.], *Don Carlos,* V, i, 8-75; *The Orphan,* IV, i, 5-16).

he cannot sleep because of a dream that a strange fury entered his house and broke the roof. To his dismay this remark merely prompts her to refer to her own dreadful dream. "Out on my fate!" he exclaims to the audience, "I have given her the occasion /How to torment me: she will tell me hers." As she begins the recital, he begs her not to proceed because he suffers "at the mention of any dream; feel how I tremble yet". Whereupon she begins to suggest a host of cures.[28]

This comic scene touches on another category: dreams used satirically, often at the expense of women. Just before Antonio's portentous "revenge" vision in Marston's *Antonio's Revenge,* Nutriche, an attendant, describes to Lucio – the object of her amorous designs – a dream in which she was married and going to bed with him. This comic relief in prose is part of the stock joke that single women experience erotic dreams.[29] Wycherly's *Gentleman Dancing Master* carries this to the extreme of farce. The maid Prue has designs on M. de Paris, a coxcomb. Coy about a recently experienced love dream, she consents to reveal it, only after much coaxing by him:

Why then, methought last night you came up into my chamber in your shirt when I was in bed; and that you might easily do, for I have ne'er a lock to my door.

Although she blushingly protests that he can guess the rest of the dream, he insists on hearing it. She finally reveals that he joined her in bed and that she later awoke in tears, saying, "You have undone me!" She adds:

Indeed it was so lively, I know not whether 'twas a dream, or no. — But if you were not there, I'll undertake you may come when you will, and do anything to me you will, I sleep so fast.

---

[28]   Ben Jonson, *Plays,* ed. F. E. Schelling (London, 1910), *The Case Is Altered,* V, i, 2; *Epicoene,* IV, i; *Volpone,* III, ii.

[29]   Marston, I, ii, 31-40. For other examples of the joke see Webster's *White Devil,* V, iii (p. 156), and Thomas Randolph, *Poems,* ed. J. J. Parry (New Haven, 1917), pp. 54, 100.

M. de Paris is so dense that her suggestions escape him. She therefore hints further:

But now I have told your worship my door has neither lock nor latch to it, if you would be so naughty as to come one night, and prove the dream true — I am so afraid on't.

In his obtuseness he thinks he reassures her by saying, "Ne'er fear it: – dreams go by contraries." Fearful lest this be only too true, she deliberately – and amusingly – misinterprets: "Then, by that I should come into your worship's chamber and come to bed to your worship." She next attempts to capitalize on this new turn in the discussion:

Prue. But if I should do such a trick in my sleep, your worship would not censure a poor harmless maid, I hope? For I am apt to walk in my sleep.

Mons. Well, then, Prue, because thou shalt not shame thyself, poor wench, I'll be sure to lock my door every night fast.

By this time fully exasperated, she is about to be direct and explicit with him when they are interrupted.

Wycherly even went beyond the world of maidservants and applied this stock situation to the more refined ladies of the main plot. The heroine confesses to her aunt, "an impertinent precise old woman", that she has had impure dreams of a man. The aunt, deprecating dreams, admits that the experience is common, "for you must know, widows are mightily given to dream" and dreams are "waggishly called 'widow's comfort' ". When the heroine retorts that she was pleased with her dream, the aunt adjudges this still no infringement of modesty. The heroine therefore teases her: "Ay; but to be delighted when we wake with a naughty dream, is a sin, aunt; and I am so very scrupulous, that I would as soon consent to a naughty man as to a naughty dream." Wycherly obviously derived pleasure in having two respectable society ladies arguing about scabrous dreams.[30]

---

[30] William Wycherly, *Plays,* ed. W. C. Ward (New York, 1949), IV, i; I, i.

C. SEVENTEENTH-CENTURY NARRATIVES

When we approach the narrative works of the seventeenth century, we are somewhat surprised by the archaic flavor of the dreams. We saw in the lyric tradition examples of fine dream poems, whether judged as minute allegories or as realistic representations of desire and wish-fulfillment. The narrative dreams, however, are (except for Milton's) somewhat disappointing. Although well done, they do not come up to the spare, haunting quality achieved by non-literary people – Dorothy Osborne, Pepys, Laud – who simply wrote down what happened to them and yet seem convincing and affecting. An examination of the memoirs of such persons, moreover, reveals that they regarded dreams, even strange ones, with considerable indifference or skepticism. The theoretician, to be sure, might defend some elaborate traditional hypothesis, but what men like Feltham and Browne had in common was a sense that the age in which the validity of a dream was readily established had long since passed. Even among the religious figures of the age, only a non-conformist – in the broadest sense – like Fox could be dogmatic about seeing the hand of God or Satan in his dream experiences; an archbishop like Laud was silent. Yet in the major narrative works, the dreams are almost all objective, monitory, and supernatural, often caused by the Devil. Their major purpose seems to be to account, in the primitive manner, for an inexplicable act. One possible reason for the discrepancy between the skepticism on this subject found in seventeenth-century life (and much theory) and the prevalence of objective dreams in seventeenth-century narrative is that the epics of this period were often set in Biblical times, when supernatural dreams were a part of the spiritual landscape.

The validity of the supernatural dream is vouched for by Christiana in *Pilgrim's Progress II:*

We need not, when a-bed, lie awake to talk with God. He can visit us while we sleep, and cause us then to hear his voice. Our heart ofttimes wakes when we sleep; and God can speak to that either by words, by proverbs, by signs and similitudes, as well as if one was awake.[31]

---

[31]   John Bunyan, *Pilgrim's Progress* (Oxford, 1902), p. 220.

We have seen in Chapter III how within the vision frame of this work is embedded a single narrative dream – experienced by the man in Interpreter's House – which functions as symbolic center of the work. Similarly in Part II, Christiana's change of life is compelled by a triple dream which continues to reverberate through the rest of the narrative.[32]

The divinely inspired dream could, however, be simulated and exploited. One interesting use of a feigned dream occurs in Dryden's fable of the swallows in the *Hind and the Panther*. The swallows (Roman Catholics) think the time propitious to move southwards; the Martin (an intriguing priest) advises them to remain. "To strengthen this", he tells "a boding dream", in order to intimate slily some secret revelation of their fate. Although the swallows shake for fear of the related dream, some of the devouter ones reply, giving better reasons for leaving; faced with the authority of the alleged dream, they try to discredit it:

But, least of all philosophy presumes
Of truth in dreams, from melancholy fumes:
Perhaps the Martin, hous'd in holy ground,
Might think of Ghosts that walk their midnight round,
Till grosser atoms, tumbling in the stream
Of fancy, madly met, and clubbed into a dream.

We have here, as in the "Nun's Priest's Tale" – which Dryden translated – a beast fable with dramatic tension over the interpretation of a dream, although in this case a feigned one. The Martin and his dream win the day, but the swallows lose their lives by heeding his advice.[33]

More common than the divine or feigned dream was the in-

---

[32]   *Ibid.*, pp. 175-76, 178-79, 181, 194, 202-203, 219-220.
[33]   John Dryden, *Poetical Works*, ed. G. R. Noyes (Cambridge, Mass., 2nd ed., 1950), p. 241, 11. 1774-1812. In his translation of Chaucer's "Nun's Priest's Tale", Dryden adds a long skeptical passage that has no authority in Chaucer (p. 826, 11. 323-341). For other skeptical references by Dryden to dreams see pp. 275, 835, 837.
For miscellaneous uses of the dream in narrative works see, e.g., Giles and Phineas Fletcher, *Poetical Works*, ed. F. S. Boas (Cambridge, 1908-1909), I, 176-177, 46-47; II, 145.

fernal; an example of it of great importance in the epic narratives of the age is found in Crashaw's free translation from Marino, *Slaughter of the Innocents*. Tormented by knowledge of the birth of Christ, Satan spurs Vengeance to action. She flies down to Bethlehem, where Herod sleeps that night, and assumes the ghostly appearance of the king's dead brother Joseph. Chilling his spirit with her story, she urges him to awaken because a conspiracy is under way that will be led by a baby now born. After changing her tone to imprecation, she applies to his heart a snake which diffuses poison through him. As she leaves, Herod awakens in fear and cries for his arms in rage. Since this dream is but the climax of a series of omens, he summons his counsellors in the morning.[34]

Such a scene recurs in other major seventeenth-century narratives. A character who is becoming evil experiences an objective dream caused by Satan, often through an emissary. Desirous of foiling God's plan as carried out by good men, Satan resorts to circuitous means like the dream. For the same reason, the emissary who causes and appears in the vision usually assumes the deceptive guise of someone known to the dreamer. Standing near the bed, this "ghost" urges the dreamer to awaken, imparts some facts mixed with lies, infuses poison into his heart (often by means of snakes), and disappears while the dreamer awakens in a rage for violence.

The convention goes back at least as far as Virgil. In *Aeneid* VII, Alecto is sent by Juno to rouse Turnus to a war on the arriving Trojans. While, in Homer, Juno had been simply one goddess with interests which happened to run counter to those of Zeus and Athene, her behavior in Virgil constitutes a dissent from some sort of cosmic order. Under the Christian dispensation, the cosmic order was no longer a sensitive pagan's velleity but an established belief. Dreams of this kind became infernal – part of the Devil's grand plan to foil God and the good. We have seen several such in Tasso, for instance, as when Alecto incites

[34]   Richard Crashaw, *Works*, ed. L. C. Martin (Oxford, 1956), pp. 122-25.

Solyman or causes Christian soldiers to rebel against Godfrey.[35]

In the economy of the story such an event accounts for seemingly irrational behavior in the manner of primitive psychology (as we saw in Chapter II). Why should Herod want to kill Christ, or Saul David? The dream fills a lacuna in motivation. It is a way of presenting in palpable dramatic form the inner promptings of a divided or malicious mind. It displays man in the act of reaching a decision. Although urging action, it does not hinder free will; yet the dreamers obey the evil dreams without questioning authenticity or provenience.[36]

Crashaw's contemporary and friend, Cowley, used the same sort of incident in the *Davideis* to elucidate Saul's hatred of David. The king of Israel has been reconciled with his leading warrior and singer. Hell's forces do not approve of the accord, because "from mans agreement fierce alarms they take". An Infernal Council, called by Lucifer to solve the problem, despatches Envy earthwards to realize a plot she has proposed. Entering the sleeping king's room in the form of Father Benjamin – Jacob's son and Saul's ancestor – she approaches Saul's side, urges him to arise, informs him of David's growing power and popularity, and incites him to murder.

> With that she takes
> One of her worst, her best beloved Snakes,
> Softly dear Worm, soft and unseen (said she)
> Into his bosom steal, and in it be my Vice-Roy. . . .
> The infected King leapt from his bed amazed,
> Scarce knew himself at first, but round him gazed

---

[35] See Chapter II, Section E, for the discussion of Tasso, as well as of Homer, who is the ultimate source of this genre.

[36] The *topos* of this incident can be detected even when the dream is absent. In Phineas Fletcher's *Locusts* (*Works,* I, 164-65), the infernal spirit enters Pope Paul's chamber and fills the pontiff's breast with pride and rage, whereupon Paul calls a conclave of Cardinals. While it is not clear that the Pope is asleep, the scene is similar to that of Alecto's incitement of Argillan and Solyman (in Tasso), Vengeance's incitement of Herod, Envy's of Saul (in Cowley, *infra*), Satan's of Eve – in each case a morally indifferent or potentially good person is precipitated into evil action by the visitation.

And started back at piec'd up shapes, which fear
And his distracted Fancy painted there.

Cursing himself for having been a pious fool, he swears to kill
David. Thus is another irrational change of mind again accounted
for by an infernal dream. In his learned notes, Cowley presents
the *raison d'être* of the dream-phantom's disguise:

No person is so improper to perswade man to any undertaking, as the
Devil without a disguise: which is the reason why I make him here
both come in, and go out too in the likeness of Benjamin, who as the
first and chief of Sauls progenitors, might the most probably seem
concerned for his welfare, and the easiliest to be believed and obeyed.[37]

Cowley balances this infernal dream with a celestial one sent to
David. His epic thus depicts the struggles of Biblical men as part
of the cosmic war between good and evil. Men are the soldiers
who, receiving directions from distant headquarters, do the
battling; the dreams are the messengers. Hence, right after Saul's
dream in Book I, an angel flies down from a conference in
Heaven to the sleeping David and urges him to awaken and flee.

Up leapt Jessides, and did round him stare;
But could see nought; for nought was left but air,
Whilst this great Vision labours in his thought,
Lo, the short Prophesie t'effect is brought.

That is, he is sent for by the king to appease, with his Lyre,
"th'obscure fantastick rage of Sauls disease", which has been
generated by the infernal dream. The hero obeys instead the
vision's mandate to flee.[38]

After his tender parting from Jonathan in Book II, David
rests during his flight. By God's command thick mists arise and
put him to sleep. There follows an allegorical description of the
mind, preparatory to the account of another dream. A place
("The Head, seat of Fancie") that rears man high is the seat of

[37] Abraham Cowley, *Works,* ed. A. R. Waller (Cambridge, 1905-1906),
II, 242-44, 247-250, 272.
[38] *Ibid.,* p. 252. See also p. 264 for the regimen in force at the Prophets'
College for the purpose of obtaining mantic dreams.

the small world's heaven, where Reason moves the sphere. There also, however, rides "Phansie, wild dame", accompanied by lascivious pride, chameleons, and throngs of airy forms. These discrete images are shaped with "fit choice" by an angel sent from God to give David a mantic dream. After exhibiting the hero in kingly state among his tribes, the dream deals with the wars of establishment and consolidation, and the succession of the kings of Israel. Such a dream of posterity – of the warriors and kings to spring from the dreamer's loins – had also become traditional, the latest example to be found in the *Faerie Queene* (V, vii, st. 12-23).

Since Cowley, as a story teller, must not let us forget the over-all setting, he periodically reminds us of the dreamer. As the setbacks of one of the Israelite kings is shown, "ev'n David in his dream does sweat and shake". When the idols are cast down, David's joy grows so unruly that his sleep's silken chains barely hold him down; the angel has to stir his humours and raise more mists to seal fast his eyes. As the dream concludes, with the Virgin and angels singing Hallelujah, David awakens out of sheer joy. Everything vanishes.

Fixt with amaze he stood; and time must take,
To learn if yet he were at last awake.
Sometimes he thinks that heaven this Vision sent,
And ordered all the pageants as they went.
Sometimes, that onely 'twas wild Phancies play,
The loose and scattered reliques of the Day.

Dressing himself in thickened air, Gabriel comes to inform David that what he had seen was the truth "shaped in the glass of the divine foresight".[39]

That Cowley utilized two traditional types of celestial dreams – of warning and of posterity – in addition to the usual infernal kind,[40] indicates the rigidity of literary conventions even in an

[39] *Ibid.*, pp. 295-304.
[40] Other dreams in seventeenth-century narratives are in Butler's *Hudibras* (pp. 169, 231-38), Kynaston's *Leoline* (in Saintsbury, II, 89-90, 134-37), Chalkhill's *Theacles* (*ibid.*, 426-29, 404), Chamberlayne's *Pharonnida* (*ibid.*, I, 151-52).

age of great intellectual ferment and change. We must not be surprised therefore to find the same supernatural objective dreams again in the Biblical epic of the greatest seventeenth-century poet.

VI

MILTON

A. MILTON ON DREAMS

Milton did not utilize so many dreams in his poetic corpus as, say, Cowley or Herrick. Yet his few examples, drawing upon the traditional genres, were well chosen and meticulously realized, with that profound erudition, catholicity of taste, and painstaking craftsmanship characteristic of all his work. His responses to dreams, however, are ascertainable with difficulty because he rarely expressed himself directly on the subject. Of his voluminous prose works – which we shall examine before the poetry – only the *History of Britain* touches on the subject more than once. His deliberate studies in early English history brought to his attention many stories of the visions of early monks and saints which probably seemed to him no different from the dreams of pagan liars or contemporary "saints".

One dream related in the *History* Milton accepted wholeheartedly. The good King Edward saw in a slumber before his death two monks appearing as messengers from God to foretell that, because all the prominent persons of England were evil, God had delivered the land to their enemies. While people trembled on hearing of this incident, the "simonious" archbishops laughed at it as a feverish dream of a doting old man. "But", said Milton, "the event prov'd it true." He probably found this dream acceptable because it had a quasi-Biblical ring to it. It struck, moreover, a note characteristic of the whole book. Although he had begun the *History* as a research task for the projected Arthurian epic, he soon found himself interested in and depressed by the parallel between the sins and misfortunes of the Anglo-Saxons and the dislocation of his own time. The Bible provided another analogue – the punishment of ancient Israel for its misdeeds. The dream of Edward was therefore a prophetic warning dream in the manner of Scripture and, though it happened in pre-Conquest England, was applicable as well (especially with its glance at the simoniacal clergy) to contemporary England.

Yet throughout the rest of this work, Milton found little other dream lore acceptable. In fact disgust with the superstitious and undependable "monkish" early historians who were his only sources aroused his amusing sarcasm. William of Malmesbury, for instance, related that Athelstan's mother dreamed as a girl that she would bring forth a moon to enlighten the whole land; hearing of this, the king's nurse caused the girl – a farmer's daughter – to be brought up at court, where the king eventually married her and begat the famous Athelstan. Of the story Milton remarked that this was how a song went in William's day, "for it seems he refused not the authority of Ballats for want of better".

According to the legendary founding of Britain, Brutus, sleeping before the altar of Diana, was in a dream informed of the western isle and of the great power it would some day be. He consequently travelled west "guided now, as he thought, by divine conduct"; but Diana, Milton added caustically, overshot her oracle by saying that the whole earth would be subjected to this isle. Similarly, the story of an archbishop whipped in a dream by St. Peter for wanting to leave England Milton recounted with a qualification: "If it be worth believing"; Guthred was a servant made king by the command of St. Cudbert in a vision – "if we beleeve Legends".[1]

Milton's irreverence did not stop with superstitious monks. In the *Areopagitica* he even reexamined St. Jerome's dream, one of the most famous in Christendom. He suggested that the story of the Devil's whipping Jerome may have been a "phantasm bred by the fever which had then seized him".[2] Since Milton's

---

[1] John Milton, *Works* (Columbia University Press, N.Y., 1931-1940), X, 12, 151, 193, 231, 237, 306.
[2] *Ibid.*, IV, 307-308. We note here that he has changed the original story

burden here was to assert the right to read almost all books, he had to meet Jerome's rejection of Cicero's works and therefore readily questioned the validity of the saint's story of his dream.

This was as far as Milton could go with his skepticism in the matter and still remain a devout Christian. In the *Christian Doctrine* under the heading of "[the new dispensation] written in the hearts of the Believers", he placed among the collated passages the famous one in Joel ii which caught the imagination of the seventeenth century, "Your young men shall see visions, and your old men shall dream dreams." Milton's comment was: "For although all real believers have not the gift of prophecy, the Holy Spirit is to them an equivalent and substitute for prophecy, dreams, and visions." This passage implicitly accepts at least some prophetic dreams as valid.[3]

Furthermore, skeptical though he may have been about other people's dreams, Milton seems to have made rather lofty claims for his own as a source of inspiration. Ennius and others had presented similar claims; few did so in modern times. Yet, because such assertions were made at various stages of Milton's career, they cannot be dismissed as "imitation" of the ancients. In "Ad Patrem", for instance, he reckons that all he possesses is as nothing except for what has been the "fruit of dreams in a remote cavern and of the laurel groves of the sacred wood and of the shadows of Parnassus". In the "Fifth Elegy", he welcomes the spring because with it returns his inspiration; at night in his dreams, driven by inner flames, he is beside the Muses' stream of Pirene. As Apollo appears,

my mind is being borne up into the sheer liquid heights of the sky and, quit of the body, I go through the wandering clouds ... through shadows and grottoes, the secret haunts of the poets; and the innermost

---

- of Jerome's being called to account in Heaven, i.e., in a divine dream - into that of an infernal dream. This seems to have been part of his interest in infernal or anxiety dreams, an interest manifest also in Prolusion I (XII, 143) and the Commonplace Book (XVIII, 205, 232), as well as in *Paradise Lost* and *Paradise Regained (infra)*.

[3]   *Ibid.*, XVI, 119.

shrines of the gods are open . . . and the unseen infernal world is not impervious to my eyes.[4]

We have here the Neoplatonic wandering of the soul in dreams, a rare example of it in Milton's works.

Even if we disregard these early references as youthful rhetoric, we still face the claim twice repeated in his *magnum opus.* In the invocation of Book Three, he speaks of his nocturnal journeys to the haunt of the Christian muses, presumably for inspiration: "Thee Sion and the flowery Brooks beneath . . . Nightly I visit" (1. 32). In book Seven he addresses Heavenly Urania: "Thou /Visit'st my slumbers Nightly, or when Morn/Purples the East" (11. 29-31). These references culminate in the explicit remark in Book Nine, when he speaks of Urania, his celestial Patroness, who

> deigns
> Her nightly visitation unimplor'd,
> And dictates to me slumb'ring, or inspires,
> Easy my unpremeditated verses. (11. 21-24)

We have no way of knowing whether this intimates that he experienced an objective dream in which a spirit actually presented him with the lines; or that the lines formed themselves in dreams, and "celestial Urania" was merely a Christian poet's way of accounting for them; or that he did not dream at all, but arose full of inspiration which – following a literary convention – he attributed to an activity, in conjunction with Urania, of the soul liberated from the body.

B. MILTON'S USE OF DREAMS

On turning from these somewhat nebulous remarks about dreams to Milton's use of them in his early poems, the reader may discern a sense of the enchantment of dreams. The persona of "L'Allegro"

---

[4] Milton, *Complete Poems and Major Prose,* ed. Merritt Y. Hughes (New York, 1957), p. 83, 11. 15-16; p. 38, 11. 10-35.

loses himself in the panorama of "such sights as youthful poets dream/On Summer eves by haunted stream" (11. 129-130). Whether he means dreams literally or only daydreams, something ethereal and exotic was intended here. Since Il Penseroso thrives best at night, he hides during the day in a shady arbor, going to sleep with a wish:

And let some strange mysterious dream
Wave at his Wings in Airy stream,
Of lively portraiture display'd,
Softly on my eyelids laid. (11. 146-150)

Not concerned with such complicated matters as dreams celestial or infernal, "humorous" or "animal", mantic or vain, the poet delights in the sheer pleasure of the dream experience and hopes to awaken with music all about him.

In "Comus" a loftier view of dreams is expressed. The Elder Brother, lulling the second Brother, speaks of the security of the chaste soul: it is lackeyed by a thousand angels who drive off things of sin, "and in clear dream and solemn vision/Tell her of things that no gross ear can hear" (11. 457-458). This remark, implying that celestial dreams are still available to man, approximates Eve's words at the end of *Paradise Lost:* "For God is also in sleep, and Dreams advise" (XII, 611).

From these casual references, I pass to Milton's use of a specific dream. To the genre of vision poems, he devoted his "Elegy III", mourning the death of the Bishop of Winchester. The poet, grief stricken by a waking vision of the plague and the resultant fatalities, retires to bed lamenting still the Bishop's decease. He dreams of a broad field where everything is green and silver amid Elysian fragrances and sounds. The Bishop appears in his robes and, walking into the applause and embraces of heavenly presences, is invited to enter the delights of his father's kingdom. As the harps ring out, the poet awakes and weeps that the dream had vanished with the night.[5]

In its content the poem resembles "Lycidas" – and, for that

---

[5]   *Ibid.,* pp. 22-23.

matter, Drummond's *Cypress Grove* – in that the first part of the work dramatizes the difficulties of earthly life, represented in this case by the plague epidemic. The second part, again as in the "Lycidas" genre, complements the view of this life with a vision of the hereafter. Both realms are parts of reality to the Christian, but since suffering is self-evident while the hereafter is a matter of faith, Milton utilizes the dream to represent the latter. As in Drummond's work, the dream encloses the supernatural, the invisible, the numinous – what we see through a glass darkly. Thus the elegy, ostensibly a lament for one man, takes up, as all great poems must, the larger questions of life. The Bishop functions as a link; because the poet mourned him during waking hours, his dream has a naturalistic basis. Milton thereby attains a better fusion of the two halves than exists in Drummond's unexplained sorrow and vision; Milton's experience adheres to the traits of the natural dream even while its content is supernatural.

Natural and supernatural are strangely mingled as well in Milton's superb love-dream lyric, Sonnet 23.

> Methought I saw my late espoused Saint
>> Brought to me like Alcestis from the grave,
>> Whom Jove's great Son to her glad Husband gave,
>> Rescued from death by force though pale and faint.

She appears purified of all taint "and such, as yet once more I trust to have/Full sight of her in Heaven without restraint". These last two lines are rich in emotion but of ambiguous import. They may be a recollection of the veiled Alcestis in Euripides's tragedy, or a statement by a Petrarchan lover of his faith in a reunion with his beloved. If the lady in question, however, is Milton's second wife, whom the blind poet never saw, the desired "full sight of her" carries a special impact. The next four lines raise the problem again:

> Came vested all in white, pure as her mind:
>> Her face was veil'd, yet to my fancied sight,
>> Love, sweetness, goodness, in her person shin'd
> So clear, as in no face with more delight.

Does "fancied sight" refer to something seen in "fancy" (i.e., dream), or to the fact that her face was by his blindness veiled from him in life, that he did not and would not know what it looked like until his own death? Her silent presence in the dream adds to the mystery of the experience. In the last lines comes the usual yet touching attempt to unite:

But O, as to embrace me she inclin'd,
I wak'd, she fled, and day brought back my night.[6]

Although thousands of love-dream lyrics conclude in this fashion, Milton somehow generates new power from an old idea while using the simplest language and syntax.

The ambiguities, which render precise interpretation difficult, have been much debated. The poem is in fact powerful because all the interpretations are acceptable: it moves on several levels. It may be an impersonal sonnet to the angelified lady, in the tradition of Dante and Petrarch; she reappears after death to comfort her lover, as in Petrarch's or Drummond's sonnets. The references to sight need not indicate the blind poet at all, since the concluding remark, "day brought back my night", is one of the old paradoxes of the love-dream tradition. To the lover – everything being turned upside-down and inside-out – the world cannot but be dark without the lady who usually outshines the sun itself.

The poem, however, gains additional power if, like most of Milton's sonnets, it dramatizes a personal experience. In that case, the day brings back a double night: not only the figurative one of the bereft lover, but also the paradoxical waking night of the blind man who, during the real external "night", sees some things at least in dreams. The last word, "night", is thus important, since from the phrase "full sight" in line eight we obtain an ironic awareness that "night" and "fancied sight" have, besides the usual meaning, an additional significance peculiar to the blind John Milton.

From lyric, masque, vision, and sonnet we turn to the form

---

[6]   *Ibid.*, p. 170.

Milton revered most, the epic. In the early *On the Fifth of November,* the Pope goes to sleep, when Satan appears at his side dressed as a Franciscan monk. Rebuking him for slumbering while savage England mocks him, persecutes Catholics, and defeats the Armada, Satan urges the Pope to rise and act. But the pontiff is to use treachery rather than open war – as the Arch Fiend will decide also in *Paradise Lost.* While Satan flies back to Hell, the Pope awakes, turns over in his mind the delightful dream, and summons Murder, Treason, *et al.* to begin the plot.

This scene is clearly modeled on the traditional infernal dream of Christian epics, based ultimately on *Aeneid* VII. The details are in complete conformity to those on the other seventeenth-century epics of Crashaw, Cowley, and the Fletchers. The Satanic person, for instance, appears to a ruler in the guise of some-one close to him, urges action, and suggests a plot. As he vanishes, the awakened, possessed dreamer resorts to evil acts he seemingly has not thought of before; he is now motivated. Even the use of personification is traditional. With Phineas Fletcher, Milton shares as well a similarity of subject matter – although Fletcher depicts a waking "inspiration", while Milton utilizes the dream. So we see the young Milton learning his craft by writing in a mode that is of his time.[7]

The guise of the Franciscan is used by Satan again when ac-costing the waking Christ in *Paradise Regained.* His attempts at suasion failing, Satan resorts to dreams. This pattern of behavior, common in the early hagiographies, was delineated by St. Grego-ry the Great, who pointed out that, although the Devil may disturb the balance of a saint for a moment, the saint will quickly clear his mind; hence, unable to make headway with a waking man, Satan resorts to the deadlier assault in sleep, through dreams.[8]

[7] Because of Milton's long career, we may forget that his short epic an-teceded the other narratives. He wrote it in 1626, before Fletcher (1627), Crashaw (ca. 1633), and Cowley (1637-1643) wrote theirs. It seems likely that each of the four writers arrived at his dream narrative independently, although mutual influences must not be ruled out, as all four attended Cambridge.

[8] St. Gregory the Great, *Morals on the Book of Job,* trans. anon. (Oxford, 1844-1850), p. 449; a similar point is made in the anonymous fif-

The vision induced in the hungry Christ is one of wish-fulfillment, "As appetite is wont to dream,/Of meats and drinks." Ravens seem to be bringing food to Elijah, and Christ appears to join the prophet in meals brought by angels. With the dawn, Christ rises and finds "all was but a dream,/Fasting he went to sleep and fasting waked". Although we know Satan to have caused it, the vision seems to be a subjective "natural" dream from within, springing from Christ's fasting.[9]

Towards the end of the work, Satan uses the dream to frighten rather than to tempt. Christ falls asleep in the midst of storms called up by Satan: "At his head/The Tempter watch'd, and soon with ugly dreams/Disturb'd his sleep." No other details are given. Some lines later, shrieking ghosts, Furies, specters are said to surround Christ, but whether they are outside or in the dream is not clear. The detail of Satan standing at the sleeper's head is in accord with the earliest Near Eastern and Greek descriptions of objective dreams and brings us to his similar posture near Eve's ear at the time of her infernal dream in *Paradise Lost*.[10]

C. EVE'S DREAM

In Eve's dream someone appears to be at her ear telling her in a gentle, Adam-like voice to walk abroad. Describing rhapsodically the evening's attractions, the voice intimates Nature's desire to

---

teenth-century work, *Malleus Maleficarum*, trans. M. Summers (London, 1928), p. 54.

[9] *Paradise Regained*, II, 260-283. For this kind of natural dream, see Is. xxix. 7-8.

[10] *P.R.*, IV, 407-409, 422-431. It seems curious that Milton used the infernal dream more than the other kinds. He was certainly interested in it: we have already seen that, deliberately or through forgetfulness, he altered St. Jerome's dream into an infernal one. Indeed in *P.R.* itself (I, 392-96), Satan informs Christ that he (Satan) dwells co-partner with man in the regions of this world, even aiding and advising man through dreams. Thus the famous dream of Eve, without Scriptural documentation or other source, springs out of Milton's active interest in the infernal dream as a literary device, as well as out of a belief in its actuality as a phenomenon of life – a necessary corollary to the belief in the existence of Satan.

behold her. She seems to rise but does not see Adam; walking out to look for him, she finds herself suddenly at the Tree of Forbidden Knowledge, which appears even more enticing than it did by day. An angel stands near it. After wondering aloud why the tree's special powers are neglected, he tastes the fruit, praises its ability to make gods of men, and offers it to her as a means of rising to heaven like a goddess. When the savory scent of the fruit quickens her appetite, she finally eats of it. She seems then to fly among the clouds with him, to wonder at her exaltation. As her guide suddenly vanishes, she sinks down and falls asleep. "O how glad I wak'd/To find this but a dream."

Eve prefaces her narration to Adam by mentioning that the experience differed from the dreams she had known so far. It was *not* a dream, "as I oft am wont, of thee" (the love dream), nor of "works of day past" (the "animal" dream reflecting waking thoughts), nor of "morrow's next design" (the dream of wish fulfillment), but of "offense and trouble" (an anxiety dream). In a sense it foreshadows all such anxiety dreams to take place after the Fall and the attendant feelings of lustfulness, shame, guilt; the post-lapsarian "grosser sleep" – as against the pre-lapsarian "aery light sleep" – is bred of unkindly fumes, "with conscious dreams/ Encumbered".

Eve's dream is, however, pre-lapsarian and therefore not to be accounted for by such causes alone. Satan, we know from Book IV, generated it:

Assaying by his Devilish art to reach
The Organs of her Fancy, and with them forge
Illusions as he list, Phantasms and Dreams.[11]

Without a direct source in earlier literature, his dream corresponds to the first of two temptations which Eve was by tradition said to have undergone.[12] Too fine an artist to merely repeat the

---

11 *P.L.*, V, 31-32; IV, 801-803; IX, 1049-1050.
12 Grant McColley points out that because of conflicting interpretations by various exegetes, there grew up a tradition of two temptations and two warnings, in order to accommodate differing stories of the Fall. Calvin *et al.* spoke of a first unsuccesful temptation on the day of man's creation.

testing, Milton invented the dream as a variation on his basic theme – and so we have a temptation scene taking place within the mind of the sleeping person.

Although peculiar to Milton's version of the story, the dream is not unorthodox. For example, St. Thomas Aquinas held that angels, good or bad, can move the imagination. To be sure, since the act of the cogitative faculty is subject to the will, Satan cannot inject new thoughts into the mind. He can nevertheless offer a picture to man's sense, asleep or awake, by producing all the effects which result from local movements of vital spirits or humours, and thereby stimulate man's imagination. In short, Satan influences the blood which affects the fancy; the understanding, dependent on the senses through the fancy, becomes darkened; the will is misled and consents to sin. Satan can operate either from without, by appearing in disguise and using persuasion – as he did in the Temptation – or by molding the imagination from within and arousing a passionate desire for things thought of, as in Eve's dream.[13]

Milton adhered as far as possible to the scholastic principle that angels can work only with the thoughts already present in the mind. Thus the beginning of Eve's dream – a voice urging her to look at the beauties of nature – is a refashioning of the previous day's discussion by Adam and Eve of those very beauties. In that conversation, some of Eve's divagations were apparent: after Adam told her that the night was created for rest, she hinted at the conjectural pleasure of a "walk by Moon"; she then discordantly concluded a lovely hymn of obedience to her husband by asking for whom the beauty of night was created if the only two human beings slept through it. Adam replied that "Millions of spiritual creatures walk the Earth". Hence, as the couple retired,

---

The dream, though in itself of Milton's own invention, springs out of that tradition ("Paradise Lost", *Harvard Theological Review*, XXXII [1939], p. 210 n. 137).

[13] St. Thomas Aquinas, *Summa Theologica*, trans. Fathers of the English Dominican Province (New York, 1947-1948), pp. 545, 949. For similar remarks on dreams see *Malleus*, (pp. 50, 52), and Joseph Glanvill, "Against Modern Sadducism", in *Essays* (London, 1672), p. 52.

the thoughts of night, walking, angels were present in her mind. Moreover, Eve's response, when she was "born", to her own attractiveness recurred in the dream's emphasis on her beauty. The tree appeared in the dream, of course, because it was on the couple's minds; but while in Adam's thoughts it was associated only with the prohibition, Eve regarded it as something fair – so much so that at night and in the dream it seemed even fairer than usual. These thoughts residing in Eve were manipulated by Satan, who stressed the beauty of each element in order to arouse her passion.[14]

In addition to the theological approach, Eve's dream can be analyzed as the traditional epic device – from Agamemnon's dream to the Red Cross Knight's – whereby supernatural powers influence human behavior and affect the narrative plot. It begins with a literal reflection of the present; the voice at her ear comes from the supernatural personage generating the dream and standing at the head of the sleeper in a posture natural to the conventional epic dream *daimon*. At the same time the vision reflects the prohibition of the past and exhibits the alternatives of the present. Representing Satan's first attempt on man, it is second only to the Fall itself in importance. It reveals Satan's machinations anterior to Raphael's warning and to Satan's own decisive action. After the Elysian glories of Book Four, this dream and the consequent tears, comforting, and reconciliation provide a dramatic little scene which contrasts with the idyll described so far. It looks ahead – is indeed a prelude – to the major drama still to be played out.[15]

Its mantic quality is indeed evident in the proleptic references to the Temptation and Fall of Book Nine. Satan's incarnation in the lowly toad, for example, foreshadows his occupying the body of the lowlier serpent. In the dream as well as in the actual Fall, he usurps an attractive human voice, takes advantage of Adam's absence, acts the part of a benevolent person. Most important

[14] This paragraph owes much to M. W. Bundy, "Eve's Dream and the Temptation in *Paradise Lost*", *Research Studies of the State College of Washington*, X (1942), 275-76, 280-82.
[15] This paragraph is based in part on W. B. Hunter, "Eve's Demonic Dream", *ELH*, XIII (1946), 261-62, 280-82.

of all, the seductive reasoning is similar in both cases. Eve is told that Nature worships her and wishes to behold her:

Heaven wakes with all his eyes,
Whom to behold but thee, Nature's desire,
In whose sight all things joy, with ravishment
Attracted by thy beauty still to gaze. (V, 44-47)

Thee all things living gaze on, all things thine
By gift, and Thy Celestial Beauty adore,
With ravishment beheld, there best beheld
Where universally admired. (IX, 539-542) [16]

Both Satan and the voice in the dream, wondering ironically why knowledge should be scorned and man deprived of it,[17] impute jealousy and cruelty to God:

Or envy, or what reserve forbids to taste? (V, 61)

Why then was this forbid? Why but to awe,
Why but to keep ye low and ignorant ...
Or is it envy, and can envy dwell
In heavenly breasts? (IX, 703-705, 729-30)

Tasting the fruit, the angel in the dream sways Eve by his remarks on it, even as the serpent in the Fall impresses Eve by claiming to have already eaten and been transformed by it.[18] Both voices offer it to her with the argument, in Comus's vein, that the good things are to be used and shared by gods and men.[19] In both Dream and Fall the beauty of the forbidden tree,[20] as well as the sheer sensual enticement of the fruit, is remarked:

[16] Her vanity is further flattered by Satan's use of titles and epithets (V, 74; IX, 568, 611-12, 684, 732). In both scenes, Eve comes upon the Forbidden Tree apparently by accident (V, 50-52; IX, 644-45).
[17] *P.L.*, V, 58-60; IX, 665-66.
[18] *P.L.*, V, 67-68; IX, 598-612; V, 65; IX, 890.
[19] *P.L.*, V, 67, 70, 76-81; IX, 546-48, 708-714; V, 62-63, 71-73; IX, 716-17, 720-22.
[20] *P.L.*, V, 52-53; IX, 576-580.

Even to my mouth of that same fruit held part
Which he had pluckt; the pleasant savory smell
So quick'n'd appetite, that I, methought,
Could not but taste. (V, 83-86)

Meanwhile the hour of noon drew on, and waked
An eager appetite raised by the smell
So savory of that Fruit, which with desire,
Inclinable now grown to touch or taste,
Solicited her longing eye. (IX, 739-743)

Milton thereby indicates that, in addition to the spiritual seduction, physical temptation plays an important role. In the dream she proceeds to eat the fruit without further hesitation; during the Fall, however, when her powers of reasoning are awake – although unsettled now – she first indulges in a long series of rationalizations. Only when her reason has satisfied itself, does she eat; in the dream there is no waking reason to satisfy.

The sensation of flying to the clouds and then falling is a deft realistic touch, a common factor in anxiety dreams. It is also a symbolic – the one non-literal element – enactment of the rhythm of Adam and Eve's emotions in Books Nine and Ten: acting as though drunken after the Fall, they lust and jest, riding high on a wave of *hybris*. They soon lapse, however, into emotional depths. Similarly, Adam's tender gestures in allaying Eve's anxiety and tears over the dream foreshadow the larger emotional rhythms of sin, repentance, forgiveness, reconciliation in love, and continuation of life.[21] In short, one cannot but agree with B. Rajan's remark that the dream, in addition to being effective as an omen, deft in its use of supernatural machinery, and a pretext for the faculty-psychology explanation, anticipates down to minute detail the Fall and is thereby part of the system of correspondences that ties the work together.[22]

It is ironical that Eve's dream is mantic at the same time that it is infernal. Although mantic dreams were supposed to be sent

---

[21] *P.L.*, V, 31-39; this point is made by J. H. Summers, " 'Grateful Vicissitude' in *P.L.*", *PMLA*, LXIX (1954), p. 253.

[22] B. Rajan, *"P.L." and the Seventeenth-Century Reader* (London, 1947), pp. 49-50.

by God or angels, some writers thought that the fallen angels had foreknowledge which they passed on in dreams, either to mislead good men or to reward evil ones.[23] As Milton's Satan confesses in *Paradise Regained,* he lends man

Oft my advice by presages and signs,
And answers, oracles, portents and dreams,
Whereby they may direct their future lives. (I, 392-394)

But in the case of Eve, the dream is (to use Macrobius' terminology) conditionally mantic. The possibility of infection within Eve's psyche which it reveals leads to its eventual, but not inevitable, fulfillment.

Since the dream and the Fall are so clearly related, the problem arises of whether Eve incurred any guilt as a result of the former. In fact, during the past decades, there has been controversy over the question of whether Milton, in trying to render credibly "human" the prelapsarian couple, had not inadvertently burdened them with sinful behavior before the Fall. Critics have consequently been studying the dream as one of the crucial ambiguities of the story. Arnold Stein, for example, traces the series of events – he calls them "gestures" – which mark a gradual spiritual separation of Adam and Eve. In his view the dream is the first step and the cause of the succeeding ones. As to Eve's possible guilt, Stein is careful to distinguish between states of mind. Taking note of Adam's remark that the dream is no stigma if it is "unapproved by the dreamer", he feels that Eve is not fully conscious of her own moral responsibility. While an act of will would be sin, the dream "is as yet only a hint at a flaw, an intimation of the possible".[24]

E. M. W. Tillyard brings Eve across the dividing line between innocence and guilt. To him the dream, simulating the actual

---

[23] St. Thomas, p. 443; for medieval and Renaissance iterations of this notion see A. H. Thorndike, *A History of Magic and Experimental Science* (New York, 1923-1958), VIII, 507, 535, 513; IV, 117, 121.

[24] Yet it is projected – Stein believes – by an inner conflict for which she must bear responsibility; Satan, perceiving the flaw, exploits it thereafter (Arnold Stein, *Answerable Style* [Minneapolis, 1953], pp. 83, 85-89, 93-94, 102).

Temptation, is the first stage of the Fall, for Satan insinuates into her mind the idea of allowing herself to be admired. Eve, to be sure, does not approve of the dream; yet, it touches her deeply, as is seen from the discomposed tresses, the glowing cheeks, the disquieting mood in which she awakens, and the subsequent tears. She is in a state of sin.[25]

The most extensive indictment is drawn up by Millicent Bell, who insists that the imperceptible transition from innocence to sin can be felt quite early in the poem, when "the rehearsal of the temptation presented in Eve's dream already moves her across the border this side of innocence". Miss Bell's central point is that Adam and Eve are "human" and fallen from the very start; the Fall merely brings them self-consciousness, that is, a knowledge of their own sinfulness. Milton added the ambiguous dream as but one more sign of the fallen state. To meet the theological objections to her position, Miss Bell presents as peculiar to Christianity the principle that an evil thought in itself can be an actual sin.[26]

Replying to Miss Bell, Wayne Shumaker insists on a basic distinction between merely seeing – being momentarily tempted – and acting. Even if Eve awakes from the dream in a discomposed state, she reveals her innocence and disapproval of the dream by exclaiming, "O how glad I wak'd/To find this but a dream!" The narrator's line, "So all was cleared, and to the Field they haste" – as well as his description of their praying: "innocent" – bespeaks a final dismissal of any guilt incurred. In short, sin begins not at the conception of an idea but only in the moment the will approves of it.[27]

---

25   E. M. W. Tillyard, *Studies in Milton* (London, 1951), pp. 11, 31, 70.
26   She adduces the gospel's equating with the active adulterer the man who but lusts in his heart, and St. Augustine's remark that secret ruin preceded open ruin, that the sin of the Fall began before the technical evil act (Millicent Bell, "The Fallacy of the Fall in *P.L.*", *PMLA*, LXVIII [1953], pp. 867, 871, 875, and LXX [1955], 1188, 1193-1195).
27   Or, in technical language, not at the first importunities of the concupiscent appetite but when that appetite has mastered the Will. Adam is therefore correct – Shumaker believes – in saying that sin is an act of Will. In Book Five, Eve is as yet in firm control of any evil impulse with-

H. V. S. Ogden introduces a new distinction into the discussion: Adam and Eve, as Milton describes them, are innocent and without sin, but not perfect. Her dream, her narration and rejection of it, leave her sinless yet reveal her potential weakness, even as Adam's placid reaction to the incident indicates his need for instruction by the angel. If she withstands the temptation in Book Nine, the dream will have been an important step in Satan's defeat and Eve's spiritual growth. Instead she fails; but the alternatives are open to her. Ogden accepts Stein's appellation of "gestures" for the steps to the Fall, because the word implies a distinction between a liability to sin and the commission of it, between potentiality and actuality, between the beginning of the evil will and the completion of the evil act. Such "gestures" are steps to the Temptation, but not necessarily to sin.[28]

Some years before the controversy began, M. W. Bundy shed light on the problem by adducing another theological authority – Milton's own *Christian Doctrine*. Asserting that Milton did not believe in complete innocence but in "potentially sinful thoughts before the consummation of the sin", Bundy cited a distinction drawn in Milton's tractate (I, xi) between evil concupiscence or the desire to sin and the act itself. Bundy concluded that Eve's state of mind, as illustrated by the dream, constitutes the first gradation of sin in the garden, evil concupiscence. The Temptation and Fall are the consummation or effect of this mental state.[29]

---

in her (Wayne Shumaker, "The Fallacy ..." *PMLA,* LXX [1955], pp. 1186-87, 1199, 1202).

[28] The dream is therefore both a narrative foreshadowing of the Temptation and a psychological step to it. Ogden also carries forward Shumaker's task by meeting Miss Bell's citation of St. Augustine: In the first place, Augustine had distinguished between the evil will preceding the act and the evil act itself; Milton, moreover, did not impute so great a corruption of will to the pre-lapsarian couple as did Augustine (H. V. S. Ogden, "The Crisis of *P.L.* Reconsidered", *PQ,* XXXVI [1957], pp. 2-13).

[29] Thus the dream, obtruding on the idyllic picture, brings out the potential evil lurking in Eve's curiosity and in Adam's blandness. The innocent couple is, as Ogden was later to iterate, imperfect; Satan fashions a dream out of her fancies and then continues working on an imperfect Eve set to rest by Adam's incomplete knowledge. For Bundy, in short, the dream has

These critics seem to have also ignored the relevance of the remarks of two formidable authorities, St. Gregory the Great and St. Thomas Aquinas. Gregory holds that the cause of the dream determines the degree of culpability. Only that dream which springs from waking, willing consent to unlawful thoughts is sinful. Agreeing with Gregory that the dreamer must not have done anything when awake to incur an evil vision, Thomas asserts that, since man's reason is suspended in sleep, the dreamer cannot otherwise be held responsible for any dream occurrence. Milton's Eve would certainly be guiltless by the criteria of these two thinkers, and so indeed Adam acquits her: "Which gives me hope/That what in sleep though didst abhor to dream/Waking thou never wilt consent to do.[30]

Another remark by Thomas about the relation of demon to man indirectly sheds light on the meaning of Eve's dream and on her possible guilt. Thomas asserts that demons tempt in order to know how to deceive, how to urge into sin:

The demons know what happens outwardly among men; but the inward disposition of man God alone knows. ... It is this disposition that makes man more prone to one vice than to another: hence the devil tempts in order to explore this inward disposition of man, so that he may tempt him to that vice to which he is most prone.[31]

We see therefore that Milton inserted the dream into the venerable story not only as a variation on the theme of temptation but also because it is for Satan an important test probe; it determines in fact the strategy and form of the actual – and successful – Temptation. While it leaves Eve guiltless in the eyes of God, the dream

---

an important role in the symmetry of the epic. It occurs a third of the way through the poem and represents the state of concupiscence; the Fall occurs two thirds of the way through the work and represents Actual Sin; the last third deals with Redemption (Bundy, "Eve's Dream", 290-91).

[30] St. Gregory the Great in Bede, *Works*, trans. J. E. King (London, 1930), I, 147-153; Thomas pp. 1819-1820, 2493; *P.L.*, V, 120-21.

[31] Thomas, pp. 545, 557. For a fuller discussion of the background to this question, see my "Dreams and Guilt", *Harvard Theological Review*, LVIII (1965), 69-90.

yet reveals to Satan her peculiar vulnerabilities, as well as Adam's.

The failing in Adam that Satan's bait brings out (besides uxoriousness) is *hybris*. Although saddened by the story of the ominous dream, Adam tries to explain it away by means of the faculty psychology: fancy, second to reason and in command over the five senses, mimics the sleeping reason imperfectly by matching images disjointedly,

> and most in dreams,
> Ill matching words and deeds long past or late.
> Some such resemblance methinks I find
> Of our last Evening's talk, in this thy dream,
> But with addition strange.

His observation that the dream nebulously reflects the previous day's conversation labels this a subjective "animal" vision but leaves out of account the chance that it may have been induced from without for evil purposes. Adam concludes that she should not worry over this dream, because "Evil into the mind of God or Man/May come and go, so unapprov'd, and leave/No spot or blame behind."[32] In effect, Eve's *somnium diabolicum* is explained away by Adam as a *somnium animale* – just as Chauntecleer's dream in Chaucer's "Nun's Priest's Tale" is belittled by Pertelote.[33] Adam's analysis, although a perfect summary of seventeenth-century beliefs about the "animal" dream, is irrelevant to her supernatural experience. He rules out the possibility of evil within Eve just as he ignores that of evil from without. Assuming that she is pure even though her dream is not, he is sure that what she abhors to dream of she will never consent to do awake.

---

[32]   *P.L.*, V, 31-32, 95-114, 117-9.

[33]   That is, Chauntecleer's mantic dream of unknown provenience is incorrectly and recklessly explained away by Pertelote as a *somnium naturale* (somatic), while the supernatural and mantic varieties of dreams are ignored. In *Paradise Lost*, as in the "Nun's Priests's Tale" (and *Pantagruel*), high drama is being created out of human uncertainty as to dreams. Moreover, Adam is also comparable to Chauntecleer in that uxoriousness leads both husbands to a Fall after the occurrence of a warning dream. For Chauntecleer see Chaucer, *Works,* ed. F. N. Robinson (Rev. ed., Boston, 1957), pp. 200-203.

Moreover, Adam's own earlier supernatural dream, related in Book Eight, parallels her experience; and when he awakened then, he found it to have been an accurate and truthful reflection of reality. This event alone should have put him on his guard as to the possibility of a like development in Eve's case. Eve, sensing that her dream was something beyond her normal experience, shows herself wiser in this regard than Adam, but she does not know how to analyse the matter further. His explanation allays her fears instead of putting her on guard. His behavior in this incident is part of Milton's characterization of him as potentially intellectually arrogant and uxorious. The same cocksureness leads in Book Eight to Raphael's reproof of his astronomical inquiries; the same uxoriousness present in other incidents prompts him above all else to comfort Eve and to emphasize her abhorrence of the dream-content, at the expense of her equally obvious response to it. That he does not see its true import and that his explanation is irrelevant are parts of his tragedy.[34]

The dream, then, is infernal, primarily non-symbolic, indirectly admonitory, conditionally mantic, and objective. From a modern point of view, it is also partly subjective in that it reflects some inner promptings. Prohibitions of any kind beget a restiveness and a desire to break down constraint, a desire sometimes fulfilled in dreams. We should remember Plato's remark that there is no "conceivable folly . . . not excepting . . . the *eating of forbidden food*" which a man will not commit in dreams.[35] Hence this vision, by rehearsing Eve's thoughts and insidiously extending them, functions as a wish fulfillment. The angel who eats the fruit in the dream does what she herself wants to do. Her psyche dares at first to represent the forbidden action only as undertaken by someone else. It then musters the courage to exhibit Eve herself eating the fruit in the dream. The latter dream-action is in

---

[34] This analysis of Adam is partly based on Bundy, "Eve's Dream", pp. 274, 279, 285-88.
[35] The italics are mine. Plato, "The Republic" IX, in *Dialogues*, trans. B. Jowett (New York, 1942), I, 829.

turn a preliminary venture,[36] before Eve dares to eat the fruit in actuality.

Since it brings to consciousness a potential evil act and uncovers inner promptings, this dream behaves according to the theories of Felltham and Tryon: it reveals Eve's susceptibility to the temptation awaiting her. It thereby also intensifies the reality of free will – one of Milton's basic themes. By going through the motions of sinning, Eve obtains an experiential acquaintance with the moral alternatives and bears full responsibility for her acts. Hers is not a cloistered virtue rejecting an unknown evil. In the dream, itself a temptation, she comes as close to evil as she can without actually committing it. Aware of the incipient desires within her, she should now be sufficiently disciplined to repulse the actual temptation. In providing the first temptation, Satan unwittingly cooperates with God's plan of giving Adam and Eve every possible anticipatory knowledge of the consequences of their action. If Eve had heeded the import of the dream and had been educated by its experience, she would never have failed the supreme test by falling for a seduction that followed faithfully the scenario presented in the dream.

We might ask how this infernal dream differs from the examples in Crashaw, Cowley, and the *Fifth of November*. Certainly Eve's dream evinces greater sophistication in the narration – instead of the conventional hortatory speeches from a demon, we have a fantasy of direct action; in place of an allegorical personification assuming the guise of a friend, Satan comes to Eve as a mysterious stranger. Moreover, in the earlier narratives, Herod, Saul, and the Pope are incited directly by the dream. They accept its images as real and its commands as binding. Their decisions, immediate and peremptory, to commit a sinful act have now been motivated. Such scenes are dramatic but not too convincing as human psychology. Eve, on the other hand, does

---

[36]　Stein (p. 102) believes that the dangerous state of mind of Eve is paralleled and clarified by Adam's remark about her in Book Eight: "So absolute she *seems*/And in herself complete." Eve's dream, like Adam's qualified woman worship, is "the illusion that is enjoyed in spite of formal disapproval [and it] corrupts the control of reality".

not react so at all; she remains a free agent. Instead of inserting the dream crudely as a motivating factor, Milton uses it as a warning to the couple or as an introduction to the warning soon delivered by Michael. Far from accounting completely for Eve's acts, it merely presents the possibilities open to her.

The basic difference, however, between the earlier infernal dreams and Milton's is that the others are unimaginable without the Devil, while Eve's is so natural and "realistic" that she could have dreamed it without the supernatural presence. Although the grand war between God and Satan required the latter's presence, Milton nevertheless took great pains to naturalize the dream. Such craftsmanship produced one of the most credible, subtle, and beautiful dreams in seventeenth-century literature.[37]

C. OTHER DREAMS IN *PARADISE LOST*

Eve's dream is complemented by three others in *Paradise Lost*. Book Eight, which recounts the creation of man, presents the newly "born" Adam falling asleep in the midst of wonder:

When suddenly stood at my Head a dream
Whose inward apparition gently mov'd
My fancy to believe I yet had being
And lived.

---

[37] In summary, Eve's dream has the following roots: (1) *exegetical*: the two discrete traditions of Eve's temptation fusing into a belief that she was twice tempted; (2) *theological:* the writings of Aquinas and others on Satan's probing by means of dreams; (3) *secular philosophy*: Plato's remark about the eating of forbidden food in dreams; (4) *moral:* the dream's educating Adam and Eve in the alternatives presented to their free will; (5) *esthetic*: the dream's ominous proleptic references, as well as its being a variation on the theme of temptation; (6) *literary*: the tradition of supernatural dreams as it came to Milton from the *Iliad, Aeneid*, hagiographies, *Jerusalem Delivered, The Faerie Queene,* and the seventeenth-century Biblical epics; (7) *psychological*: the verisimilitude of a quasi-anxiety dream at this juncture in the story (see my "The Anxiety Dream in Literature from Homer to Milton", *SP*, LXIV [1967], 65-82); (8) *personal*: Milton's interest in infernal dreams (see for this sections A and B above). These varied elements, brought together by the catalyst of Milton's genius, issued in Eve's dream.

That is, he retains self-awareness in the sleeping state. A divine shape, addressing Adam in the dream, leads him through the air, over fields and water, to the woody Mount of Paradise. All is beautiful there, and the lovely fruits move in him the appetite to eat. He then awakes to find everything actually before him as the dream has "lively shadowed". Even his guide appears and converses with him.[38]

This dream is noteworthy for several reasons. In the first place, it is entirely objective in that a spirit generates it and changes the dreamer's environment. Furthermore the dream, reflecting the actual incident taking place concurrently, is readily translated into reality. In this respect it is perhaps modelled on Dante's first dream in *Purgatorio,* one in which the dreamer similarly saw himself carried aloft and found on awakening that this event had indeed taken place. Thirdly, the dream parallels Eve's in several respects: the dreamer experiences the sense of flying; he comes to a lovely place where there are lovely trees; his appetite is aroused. Both are supernatural, objective dreams – one diabolic, the other divine.

But the two also contrast. Eve's dream, experienced after several days' life in the garden, is composed of the materials of her experience and perhaps of a thwarted impulse against the prohibition. The newly-created Adam's dream, without source in experience, is a divine dream sent in response to his request. Eve's dream-temptation is to present herself to nature as an object of adoration, while Adam seeks the contemplation of God. The guide reveals to the awakened Adam an object of religious devotion – the "Author of all that thou Seest" – and a token prohibition; Eve's guide, remaining within the dream, offers her forbidden fruit and incitement to disobedience. Instead of adoring God, she is herself made the object of idolatry. In short, just as the Council scene in Hell, for instance, was paralleled by the one in Heaven – the many points in common merely enhancing the important differences between good and evil – here we see good and bad versions of acts in themselves indifferent, in a studied contrast of dreams,

[38]   *P.L.,* VIII, 287-314.

voices, gardens, trees, adorations. Adam's experiences and acts superficially resemble Eve's yet are a world apart from them because guided by the divine in a celestial dream.

Soon thereafter Adam has another dream when God agrees to give him a mate. Exhausted by the unequal conversation with his Maker, he falls asleep; although his eyes are closed, the "Cell of Fancy" of his internal sight remains open. He beholds a glorious person fashion a rib into a beautiful woman. Very much as in the love-dream lyrics

Shee disappear'd, and left me dark, I wak'd
To find her, or for ever to deplore
Her loss, and other pleasures all abjure. (VIII, 478-480)

Unlike the experience of such lyrics, however, this dream turns into reality as Adam eventually finds the woman "such as I saw her in my dream". Like Adam's first vision, this is objective, celestial, literal, and reflective of present actuality.[39]

In both dreams, Adam's behavior is impelled by fancy directing his concupiscence. In the first one he wants to pluck and eat the luscious fruit; in the second he is drawn to the lovely creatures. Yet in these celestial dreams no action results because, after the sudden stir of appetite, Adam awakens as reality interrupts his normal response. His dreams have no ill effect on him, while Eve's may in some way have tainted her fancy.[40] Milton probably took a hint from Scripture for what seems to be another common denominator for Adam's pair of dreams. Both coincide with two important supernatural events: the entrance into Paradise and the creation of Eve. Perhaps Milton thought that Adam was put to

---

[39] According to W. B. Hunter ("Prophetic Dreams in *P.L.*", *MLQ* [1949], pp. 278-282), both dreams are somewhat in accord with Maimonides's third grade of prophecy, that is, they are part of a sleep in which God seems to speak to the prophet (as against the direct, first, or *gradus mosaicus,* and the second grade, of angelic appearance). The outer senses are laid to rest; the fancy alone remains active and able to see, as if through the bodily senses, but actually through reason.

[40] Murray W. Bundy – "Milton's Prelapsarian Adam", *Research Studies of the State College of Washington,* XIII (1945), p. 178 – discusses the role of concupiscence in Adam's dreams.

sleep in Genesis when woman was wrought because the supernatural cannot be beheld at first hand by even a pre-lapsarian
human being. As Michael puts it in Book Twelve: "Objects divine/
Must needs impair and weary human sense" (11. 8-9). Hence the
two events are observed in dream trances. These visions, it should
be noted, reflect the supernatural of the present but do not instruct
as to either past or future.

Adam experiences a third dream in *Paradise Lost* when Michael
is sent, after the Fall and repentance, to reveal the future history
of man. Guide and mortal ascend a hill, leaving Eve to

Sleep below while thou to foresight wak'st,
As once thou slep'st, while She to life was formed. (XI, 368-69)

Upon the hill of visions, Michael, removing from Adam's eyes
a film caused by the fruit, gives him some herbs which pierce
the inmost seat of mental sight. Rendered sensitive to incursions
of the supernatural in spite of the Fall, Adam sinks into a trance
in which he observes the pageant of human history.[41] As Adam's
mental sight begins to fail (because divine objects impair human
sense, even in dream), Michael relates the rest without recourse
to vision. This alteration is in accord with Hebrew precepts on
prophecy: Maimonides held that the experience sometimes begins
with mantic vision and is followed by abstract prophecy. Indeed
Milton compares, by allusions and references, Adam's trance
to Old Testament prophetic experiences.[42]

When the explanations are over, Michael orders Adam to
awaken Eve. The angel has calmed her with gentle dreams portending good and composing all her spirits to meek submission.
As Adam rejoins Eve, he finds her ready to receive him with
benevolent words and aware of where he has been. God has
despatched to her sorrowing weary soul some good presages in

---

[41] *P.L.*, XI, 357 ff., 412-429, 598-602, 870-71. The traditional analogues
to this dream of posterity are many: *Aeneid* VI, 754-854; *The Faerie
Queene*, III, iii, st. 29-49; *Davideis*, II.
[42] *P.L.*, XI, 214, 217; XII, 8-9; for Maimonides and prophecy see Hunter,
"Dreams", p. 280.

dreams, "for God is also in sleep, and Dreams advise". Contented at last, she is fully bound to his love.[43]

Adam's third dream differs from his previous two in not being just a reflection of the present but a visionary trance containing prophetic insight and foresight. It is Eve who now experiences the type of dream – reflecting the miraculous present – that Adam has had before. The tableau of Eve watching in a dream Adam beholding the future in a special vision is symbolic of the traditional hierarchy of the Great Chain of Being. It was sketched in Book Five when Eve retired while Raphael instructed Adam. Man, as the superior creature, receives the burden of post-lapsarian knowledge – the sad career of history – and passes the mystery on in a more casual and mitigated form to his spouse.

In another sense, their roles are reversed. Adam slept while Eve was created supernaturally, although he observed the act in a dream; now Eve sleeps while Adam is educated supernaturally and she observes him in a dream. This dream is of better portent than her first, infernal one; Adam, in turn, has moved on to experience the most special vision of the epic. In sum, *Paradise Lost* presents three kinds of dreams: one infernal;[44] three celestial dreams (two by Adam, one by Eve) that display supernatural events at the moment of their occurrence and that allow human beings to see present "mysteries" through the shielding medium of slumber; one celestial dream that is a visionary mantic trance.[45] And so, examining *Paradise Lost* by narrative rather than chronological order, we have moved to the loftiest vision – of man's anguished yet not inglorious history – from the most consequential and unfortunate infernal dream of all.

---

[43] *P.L.*, XII, 594-96, 611.

[44] With many overtones: of warning dreams; of prophesying; of reflections of past discussion, present restiveness at prohibition, and present lurking danger. It should be noted that there are no purely natural dreams in *Paradise Lost* (or in any of Milton's major works).

[45] The celestial dreams also approximate the genres of the love dream, the divine guidance dream, and the dream of posterity. Thus *Paradise Lost*, like the *Aeneid* and *Jerusalem Delivered*, has a rich variety of dream genres.

EPILOGUE

Despite monumental strides forward in all the sciences and despite the creation of supreme literary works, the seventeenth century in England did not produce any radical innovations in either the theory of dreams or in the use of dreams in literature. This is not to say that its writings on this matter are without interest. Tryon, Felltham, and Browne were carrying on the old Platonic-Stoic tradition of the dream's heuristic function, while Hobbes in effect restated Lucretius' skepticism based on atomism in terms of his own philosophy of motion. (In the wars of ideas, Hobbes' viewpoint was to become predominant.)

In literature the seventeenth century adopted and modified the traditional dream genres with varying success. The vision works, by then written mainly in prose, diminished in scope and effectiveness and ceased being an important means of expression for most writers; yet during the decline of the genre, one of the greatest of all dream visions was created – *Pilgrim's Progress*. The love dream lyrics, as widespread and well executed as ever, present excellent examples by Donne, Jonson, Herrick, Milton, and Oldham. The dreams in the drama are normally interesting and occasionally superlative, as when treated for satiric purposes by Wycherly, or for psychological and mantic purposes by Shakespeare. The supernatural monitory dreams in Biblical narrative, to be sure, seem rigid and archaic but are redeemed by Milton's paramount example, which manages to be evocative and "realistic" even while being traditionally infernal and mantic at the same time. In sum, there are occasions in this period when the dream becomes the setting for or catalyst of great literary expression: Clarence's and Lady Macbeth's dreams, as well as several of Shakespeare's metaphoric uses of the dream; Donne's and Jonson's "Dream" lyrics; Milton's Sonnet 23 and Eve's dream; *Pilgrim's Progress.* In the literature of dreams, as in other literary matters, the seventeenth century often excels by using the old well rather than by being original in the modern sense of the word.

The frequent use of dreams in seventeenth-century literature springs not only from the literary tradition developed in previous ages but perhaps also from phenomena peculiar to that epoch. Early in the century, for example, a curiosity about abnormal pathology finds expression in works like Burton's and Bright's on melancholy and in certain themes and characters in Jacobean drama. Such an intellectual *milieu* may well be responsible for the attention to dreams. Later in the century, moreover, as the Puritan movement gains momentum, there arises an interest in "enthusiasm", in frequent supernatural inspiration and personal experience of the divine. The dream is a related experience, coming from strange and mysterious sources which some persons may be too ready to connect with the divine and others as ready to satirize. Such a conjecture as to the dream's relation to the climate of ideas would account for its lesser importance during the eighteenth century and its reemergence in nineteenth-century literature.

Indeed if we momentarily glance beyond the seventeenth century to our own time, we find that the philosophy of dreams remained eclectic and bound to the past until the late nineteenth-century ferment. The Freudian revolution which then began has been the single greatest event in the history of dream lore since Hippocrates constructed the medical symbology. Working with the premise that every thought, gesture, word, and action, no matter how trivial, is revelatory of the state of one's psyche, psychoanalysis naturally finds dreams to be among the most revealing of psychic incidents. The dream, whose roots are deep in the individual's past, reveals a person's secret life.

The major difference between the modern interest in dreams and the earlier is that we turn to the dream for information about or insight into our past psychic lives, we use them as instruments of diagnosis of a present mental illness the cause of which lies in the distant past history of the psyche, whereas antiquity, the Middle Ages, and the Renaissance approached the dream for information about the body's present disposition, or for what it could tell about one's future prosperity, or for information of a theological and metaphysical nature. Basically we look to the past through the medium of the dream, the earlier ages looked to the future.

The gap between the two attitudes is nearly bridged by the tradition – partly Platonic, partly Stoic – that we may learn something about our inner selves from the dream. The expressions of this belief (by Zeno, Plutarch, Tryon, Felltham, Browne) at times would seem like anticipations of Freud were it not for the fact that the ancients are speaking of one's moral state of being rather than of psychological adjustment or of the conflict between the id and the superego.

The achievement of the Freudian revolution has been to make dreams again worthy of serious study, indeed centrally important. His theories of the unconscious have further enhanced the importance of dreams. Similarly, in literature proper, the nineteenth century saw a renewal of interest in things occult, enchanting, fantastic, exotic. Men like Coleridge, DeQuincey, Baudelaire, and Rimbaud were fascinated by dream-like trance states.

The effect of these two movements – the "scientific" and the literary – can be seen in the changes in the traditional uses of the dream. On the one hand, a work like Dickens's *Great Expectations* utilizes recurring dreams to delineate its hero as haunted by the past; the technique is at least as old as Shakespeare's *Richard III* and *Macbeth,* though Dickens multiplies the examples and makes them more "realistic", if not as poetic. In our time, this old dream-within-a-story approach is exploited in a fresh way in such motion pictures as *Wild Strawberries* and *8 1/2.*

But concurrently there have arisen, perhaps under the direct influence of Freudianism and of the literary figures mentioned before, artistic tendencies which go beyond the mere use of dreams embedded in a story or of a dream-vision frame around a series of incidents, to the total imitation of the dream state. The creations of the Surrealists – specifically of painters like

Giorgio de Chirico, Max Ernst, Salvador Dali, Kay Sage – have been matched by those of writers like Cocteau, Strindberg, Kafka, Joyce, some of whose works imitate the dream state so fully as to verge on obscurity and incoherence. Such creations are, in effect, the old dream visions but with frame and dreamer absent. These impersonal, disembodied dreams iterate the old life-is-a-dream metaphor – as used for example in Shakespeare's *Midsummer Night's Dream* and Calderon's *La vida es sueño* – but with a thoroughness and intensity that seem to deny the existence of any waking reality at all or the possibility of heuristic experience. The change is manifest also in the way the epithet "dream-like" has become honorific in our criticism of literature, painting, cinema and drama, whereas before the nineteenth century the term would normally be derogatory.

Such works and changes are valid expressions of the cultural mood of our time; the loss of belief in another and eternal world has paradoxically diminished for some thinkers the possibility of belief in the existence of this temporal world (which was heretofore considered at least an emanation from or reflection of the other). But those readers who cherish the enchantment and mystery of dreams that punctuate a clearly demarcated, fairly predictable real waking life can still turn to the dreams in seventeenth-century English literature.

BIBLIOGRAPHY

Aeschylus, *Tragedies*, trans. David Grene and Richmond Lattimore (Chicago, 1942).

Anglade, Jean, ed., *Anthologie des Troubadors* (Paris, 1927).

Apollonius of Rhodes, *Argonautica*, trans. R. C. Seaton (London, 1912).

Apuleius, *The Golden Ass*, trans. Robert Graves (New York, 1951).

Aristotle, *Parva Naturalia*, trans. W. S. Hett (London, 1935).

—, *Problems*, trans. W. S. Hett, 2 vols (London, 1937).

Armstrong, Archy, *Archy's Dreams* (London, 1641) (*Ashbee's Facsimile Reprints*, London, n.d.).

Arnold, Aerol, "Recapitulation Dream in *Richard III* and *Macbeth*", *SQ*, VI (Winter, 1955), 51-63.

Artemidoro Daldiano Philosofo Eccellentissimo dell'Interpetatione de Sogni, trans. Pietro Lauro Modonese (Venetia, 1542).

St. Athanasius, *Contra Gentes* (*Nicene and Post-Nicene Fathers*, Second Series, Vol. IV) ed. P. Schaff and H. Wace (New York, 1903).

St. Augustine, *The City of God*, trans. D. B. Zema and G. G. Walsh (New York, 1949).

Bacon, Francis, *Works*, ed. J. Spedding, R. L. Ellis, D. D. Heath, 7 vols. (London, 1857-1859).

Bede, *Opera Historica*, trans. J. E. King (London, 1930).

Behn, Aphra, *Works*, ed. Montague Summers, 6 vols. (London, 1915).

Bell, Millicent, "The Fallacy of the Fall in *Paradise Lost*", *PMLA*, LXVIII (1953), 863-883, and LXX (1955), 1187-1197, 1203.

Bland, N., "On the Muhammedan Science of Tâbír, or Interpretation of Dreams", *Journal of the Royal Asiastic Society*, XVI (1856), 118-171.

Bouché-Leclerq, A., *Histoire de la divination dans l'antiquité*, 2 volts. (Paris, 1879).

Brett, George Sidney, *A History of Psychology*, 2 vols. (London, 1912).

Bright, Timothy, *A Treatise of Melancholie* (London, 1586), ed. Hardin Craig (New York, 1940) (*Columbia University Facsimile Reprints*).

Brown, Tom, *Amusements Serious and Comical*, ed. A. L. Hayward (London, 1927).

Browne, Sir Thomas, *Works*, ed. Geoffrey Keynes, 6 vols. (London, 1928-1931).

Browne, William, *Poems*, ed. G. Goodwin, 2 vols. (London, 1894).

Büchsenschütz, Bernard, *Traum und Traumdeutung im Alterthum* (Berlin, 1868).

Bundy, Murray W., "Eve's Dream and the Temptation in *Paradise Lost*", *Research Studies of the State College of Washington*, X (1942), 273-291.

—, "Milton's Prelapsarian Adam", *ibid.*, XIII (1945), 163-184.

—, *The Theory of Imagination in Classical and Medieval Thought.* (*University of Illinois Studies in Languages and Literature*, XII, pts. 2-3, Urbana, 1927).

Bunyan, John, *Grace Abounding*, ed. G. B. Harrison (London, 1928).

—, *The Pilgrim's Progress* (London, 1902).

—, *The Pilgrim's Progress*, ed. J. B. Wharey (Oxford, 1956).

Burton, Robert, *The Anatomy of Melancholy*, ed. Floyd Dell and Paul Jordan-Smith (New York, 1927).

Butler, Samuel, *Hudibras*, ed. A. R. Waller (Cambridge, 1905).

—, *Satires*, ed. R. Lamar (Cambridge, 1928).

Calderón de la Barca, *Life is a Dream*, trans. W. E. Colford (Great Neck, N.Y., 1958).

Callimachus, *Fragments*, trans. C. A. Trypanis (London, 1958).

Carew, Thomas, *Poems*, ed. Rhodes Dunlap (Oxford, 1949).

Catullus and Tibullus, *Works*, trans. Walter K. Kelly (London, 1927).

Chapman, George, *Works*, ed. P. B. Bartlet (London, 1941).

Chaucer, Geoffrey, *Works*, ed. F. N. Robinson, Second ed. (Boston, 1957).

Cicero, *De senectute. De amicita. De divinatione*, trans. W. A. Falconer (London, 1923).

Claudian, *Works*, trans. Maurice Platnauer, 2 vols (London, 1922).

Clemen, Wolfgang, *Kommentar zu Shakespeares "Richard III"* (Göttingen, 1957).

St. Clement of Alexandria, *Christ the Educator*, trans. S. P. Wood (New York, 1954).

Coffin, Charles Monroe, *John Donne and the New Philosophy* (New York, 1958).

Colonna, Francesco, *The Strife of Love in a Dream*, trans. anon., ed. Andrew Lang (London, 1890).

Cowley, Abraham, *Works*, ed. A. R. Waller, 2 vols. (Cambridge, 1905-1906).

Crashaw, Richard, *Works*, ed. L. C. Martin (Oxford, 1956).

Cunningham, J. V., "The Literary Tradition of the Prologue to the *Canterbury Tales*", *MP* (February, 1952), 172-181.

Curry, Walter Clyde, *Chaucer and the Medieval Sciences* (New York, 1926).

Dante Alighieri, *Comedy*, trans. J. A. Carlyle, T. Okey, P. H. Wicksteed, 3 vols. (London, 1899-1901).

Denham, John, *Works*, ed. T. H. Banks (New Haven, 1928).

Diogenes Laertius, *Lives of the Eminent Philosophers*, trans. R. D. Hicks, 2 vols. (London, 1950).

Dodds, E. R., *The Greeks and the Irrational* (Berkeley, 1956).

Donne, John, *Complete Poetry and Selected Prose*, ed. John Hayward (London, 1929).

—, *Poems*, ed. Herbert J. C. Grierson, 2 vols. (Oxford, 1912).

Drummond of Hawthornden, William, *Poetical Works*, ed. L. E. Kastner, 2 vols. (Manchester, 1913).

Dryden, John, *Poetical Works,* ed. G. R. Noyes. Rev. ed. (Cambridge, Mass., 1950).

Ehrensperger, E. C., "Dreams words in OE and ME", *PMLA,* XLVI (1931), 80-88.

Elegy and Iambus. Anacreontea, trans. J. M. Edmonds, 2 vols. (London, 1931).

Felltham, Owen, *Resolves: Divine, Moral, Political* (London, Twelfth ed., 1709).

Fergusson, Francis, *Dante's Drama of the Mind* (Princeton, 1953).

Fletcher, Giles and Phineas, *Poetical Works,* ed. F. S. Boas, 2 vols. (Cambridge, 1908-1909).

Fogle, F. R., *A Critical Study of William Drummond* (New York, 1952).

Fox, George, *Journal,* ed. J. L. Nickalls (Cambridge, 1952).

F[reke], W[illiam], *Lingua Tersancta* (London, 1703).

Freud, Sigmund, *The Interpretation of Dreams,* trans. A. A. Brill (London, 1937).

—, *An Outline of Psychoanalysis,* trans. John Strachey (New York, 1949).

A Garland for John Donne, ed. T. Spencer (Cambridge, Mass., 1930).

Geer, Russel M., "On the Theories of Dream Interpretation in Artemidorus", *Classical Journal,* XXII (1927), 663-670.

The Gilgamesh Epic, trans. N. K. Sandars (London, 1960).

Glanvill, Joseph, *Essays* (London, 1676).

Gordon, R. K., trans., *Anglo-Saxon Poetry* (London, 1926).

Gottfried von Strassburg, *Tristan,* trans. A. T. Hatto (Baltimore, 1960).

The Greek Anthology, trans. W. R. Paton, 5 vols. (London, 1916).

Gregory of Tours, *History of the Franks,* trans. O. M. Dalton, 2 vols. (Oxford, 1927).

St. Gregory the Great, *Morals on the Book of Job,* trans. anon. (Oxford, 1844).

Hadas, Moses, *A History of Latin Literature* (New York, 1952).

Hélin, Maurice, ed., *La clef des songes* (Paris, 1925).

Lord Herbert of Cherbury, *Poems,* ed. G. C. Moore-Smith (Oxford, 1923).

Herodes, *Mimes,* trans. J. M. Edmonds and A. D. Knox (London, 1929).

Herodotus, *Histories,* trans. G. Rawlinson (New York, 1942).

Herrick, Robert, *Poetical Works,* ed. L. C. Martin (Oxford, 1956).

Hesiod, *Works,* trans. Richmond Lattimore (Ann Arbor, 1959).

Hill, Thomas, *The Most Pleasante Arte of the Interpretacion of Dreams* (London, 1576).

Hippocrates, *Works,* trans. W. H. S. Jones, Vol. IV (London, 1931).

Hobbes, Thomas, *Leviathan,* ed. Michael Oakeshot (Oxford, 1953).

—,*Selected Writings,* ed. F. J. E. Woodbridge (New York, 1930).

Homer, *The Iliad,* trans. Samuel Butler (New York, 1942).
    (First published in 1898, London.)

—, *The Odyssey,* trans. Samuel Butler (New York, 1944).
    (First published in 1900, London.)

Hoskyns, John, *Life, Letters, and Writings,* ed. L. B. Osborn (New Haven, 1937).

Hunter, W. B., Jr., "Eve's Demonic Dream", *ELH,* XIII (1946), 255-265.

—, "Prophetic Dreams and Visions in *Paradise Lost*", *MLQ*, IX (1949), 277-285.

James I., *Daemonologie*, ed. G. B. Harrison (London, 1924).

Jonson, Ben, *Plays*, ed. Felix E. Schelling, 2 vols. (London, 1910).

—, *Works*, ed. C. H. Herford and P. Simpson, Vol. VII (Oxford, 1941), Vol. VIII (1947), Vol. XI (1952).

Kittredge, G. L., *Chaucer and His Poetry* (New York, 1915).

Kreuzer, J. R., "Dreams in the *Boke of the Duchesse*", *PMLA, LXVI* (1951), 543-547.

Lang, Wolfram, *Das Traumbuch des Synesius von Kyrene* (Tübingen, 1926).

Langland, William, *The Vision of Piers Plowman*, trans. H. W. Wells (New York, 1945).

Longus, *Daphnis and Chloe*, trans. G. Thornley, rev. J. M. Edmonds (London, 1916).

Lovelace, Richard, *Poems*, ed. C. H. Wilkinson (Oxford, 1930).

Lucian, *Works*, trans. A. M. Harmon and K. Kilburn, 7 vols. (London, 1913-1961).

Lucretius, *De rerum natura*, trans. W. H. D. Rouse (London, 1924).

Lyra Graeca, trans. J. M. Edmonds, 3 vols., Second ed. (London, 1928).

Macrobius, *Commentary on the Dream of Scipio*, trans. William Harris Stahl (New York, 1952).

Malleus Maleficarum, trans. Montague Summers (London, 1928).

Marston, John, *Plays*, ed. H. Harvey Wood, 3 vols. (London, 1934).

McColly, Grant, "Paradise Lost", *Harvard Theological Review*, XXXII (1939), 181-235.

Meader, W. G., *Courtship in Shakespeare* (New York, 1954).

Messer, W. S., *The Dream in Homer and Greek Tragedy* (New York, 1918).

Milton, John, *Complete Poems and Major Prose*, ed. Merritt Y. Hughes (New York, 1957).

—, *Works*, 20 vols. (New York, Columbia University Press, 1931-1940).

Minor Poets of the Caroline Period, ed. George Saintsbury, 3 vols. (Oxford, 1905-1921).

More, Henry, *Philosophical Poems*, ed. Geoffrey Bullough (Manchester, 1931).

Nashe, Thomas, *Works*, ed. R. B. McKerrow, 5 vols. (London, 1958).

Nemesius of Emesa, *On the Nature of Man*, ed. W. Telfer (Philadelphia, 1955).

Nicolson, Marjorie Hope, *Science and Imagination* (Ithaca, 1956).

Norris, John, *A Collection of Miscellanies* (London, 1706).

Ogden, H. V. S., "The Crisis of *Paradise Lost* Reconsidered", *PQ*, XXXVI (1957), 1-19.

Oldham, John, *Works*, Sixth ed. (London, 1703).

Oppenheim, A. Leo, *The Interpretation of Dreams in the Ancient Near East (Transactions of the American Philosophical Society*, New Series, Vol. XLVI, pt. 3., Philadelphia, 1956).

Otway, Thomas, *Plays*, ed. R. Noel (London, n.d.).

Ovid, *Metamorphoses*, trans. Rolfe Humphries (New York, 1956).

—, *Tristia*, trans. A. L. Wheeler (London, 1931).

Paracelsus, *Selected Writings*, ed. N. Jacobi, trans. N. Guterman, Second ed. (New York, 1958).

Petrarch, *Sonnets*, trans. Joseph Auslander (New York, 1932).

Petronius, *Satyricon*, trans. William Arrowsmith (Ann Arbor, 1959).

Pindar, *Odes*, trans. Sir John Sandys, Third ed. (London, 1937).

Plato, *Dialogues*, trans. B. Jowett, 2 vols. (New York, 1937).

Pliny the Younger, *Epistles*, trans. W. Melmoth, 2 vols., Second ed. (London, 1957).

Plutarch, *The Lives of the Noble Grecians and Romans*, trans. "John Dryden", rev. A. H. Clough (New York, n.d.).

—, *Moralia*, trans. F. C. Babbitt, Vol. I (London, 1927).

Propertius, *Works*, trans. J. S. Phillimore (Oxford, 1906).

Prudentius, *Works*, trans. H. J. Thomson, 2 vols. (London, 1949).

Rabelais, *Works*, trans. T. Urquhart and P. Motteux, 3 vols. (Oxford, 1934).

Rajan, B., *"Paradise Lost" and the Seventeenth-Century Reader* (London, 1947).

Randolph, Thomas, *Poems*, ed. J. J. Parry (New Haven, 1917).

Rauh, Sister Miriam J., *Shakespeare's Use of the Arts of Language* (New York, 1947).

Remains of Old Latin, trans. E. H. Warmington, 3 vols. (London, 1935).

Richey, M., ed. and trans., *Medieval German Lyrics* (London, 1958).

Robinson, James Harvey, *Petrarch* (New York, 1901).

Sarton, George, *Introduction to the History of Science*, 3 vols. (Baltimore, 1927-1947).

Scot, Reginald, *The Discoverie of Witchcraft* (London, 1584), ed. Montagne Summers (Bungay, Suffolk, 1930).

Sensabaugh, G. F., *That Grand Whig Milton* (Stanford, 1952).

Shakespeare, William, *Complete Works*, ed. Hardin Craig (New York, 1951).

Shumaker, Wayne, "The Fallacy of the Fall in *P.L.*", *PMLA*, LXX (1955), 1185-1187, 1197-1202.

Silver Poets of the Sixteenth Century, ed. Gerald Bullett (London, 1947).

Spenser, Edmund, *Complete Poetical Works*, ed. R. E. Neil Dodge (Boston, 1908).

Stambler, Bernard, *Dante's Other World* (New York, 1957).

Stein, Arnold, *Answerable Style* (Minneapolis, 1953).

Steiner, Hans Rudolf, *Der Traum in der "Aeneis"* (Noctes Romanae, Vol. 5, Berne, 1952).

Struve, Jürgen, *Das Traummotiv im Englischen Drama des XVII. Jahrhunderts* (Heidelberg, 1913).

Suckling, Sir John, *Works*, ed. A. H. Thompson (London, 1910).

Summers, J. H., " 'Grateful Vicissitude' in *Paradise Lost*", *PMLA*, LXIX (1954), 251-264.

Synesius of Cyrene, *Essays and Hymns*, trans. Augustine Fitzgerald, 2 vols. (London, 1930).

Tasso, Torquato, *Jerusalem Delivered*, trans. Edward Fairfax, ed. H. Morley (London, 1890).

St. Thomas Aquinas, *Summa Theologica*, trans. Fathers of the English Dominican Province, 3 vols. (New York, 1947-1948).

Thorndike, Lynn, *A History of Magic and Experimental Science*, 8 vols.
(New York, 1923-1958).

Tillotson, Geoffrey, "Dreams in English Literature", *London Mercury*,
XXVII (1933), 516-523.

Tillyard, E. M. W., *Studies in Milton* (London, 1951).

Traherne, Thomas, *Centuries, Poems, and Thanksgivings*, ed. H. M. Margoliouth, 2 vols. (Oxford, 1958).

Tryon, Thomas, *A Treatise of Dreams and Visions*, Second ed. (London,
1695).

Valerius Flaccus, *Argonautica*, trans. J. H. Mozley (London, 1934).

Vaschide, N. and H. Pieron, "Prophetic Dream in Greek and Roman Antiquity", trans. T. J. McCormack, *The Monist*, XI (January, 1901), 161-
194.

Vaughan, Henry, *Works*, ed. L. C. Martin, Second ed. (Oxford, 1957).

Virgil, *The Aeneid*, trans. L. Hart and V. R. Osborn (New York, 1882).

Waller, Edmund, *Poems*, ed. G. Thorn Drury, 2 vols. (London, 1904).

Walther von der Vogelweide, *Sprüche. Lieder. Der Leich*, ed. Paul Stapf
(Berlin, 1955).

Webster, John, *The White Devil*, ed. J. R. Brown (Cambridge, 1960).

Wehrli, Max, ed., *Deutsche Lyrik des Mittelalters* (Zürich, 1955).

Weidhorn, Manfred, "The Anxiety Dream in Literature from Homer to
Milton", *Studies in Philology*, LXIV (January 1967), 65-82.

—, "Dreams and Guilt", *Harvard Theological Review*, LVIII (January
1965), 65-90.

—, "Eve's Dream and the Literary Tradition", *Tennessee Studies in Literature*, XII (1967), 39-50.

Wilmot, John Earl of Rochester, *Works*, ed. John Hayward (London, 1926).

Wither, George, *Poems*, ed. F. Sidgwick, 2 vols. (London, 1902).

Wycherly, William, *Plays*, ed. W. C. Ward (New York, 1949).

Xenophon, *Cyropaedia*, trans. Walter Miller, 2 vols. (Cambridge, Mass.,
1947).

INDEX

C4